PROSPERITY EDUCATION

GET IT WRITE!

The Ultimate Guide to **Academic Writing**

second edition

Leigh Pearson

© Leigh Pearson 2023

Prosperity Education Ltd.
Registered offices: Sherlock Close, Cambridge
CB3 0HP, United Kingdom

First published 2021
Revised edition published 2023

ISBN: 978-1-915654-15-1

This publication is in copyright. Subject to statutory exception and to the provisions of relevant collective licensing agreements, no reproduction of any part may take place without the written permission of Prosperity Education.

The moral right of the author has been asserted.

For further information and resources, visit:
www.prosperityeducation.net

To infinity and beyond.

Contents

Introduction   iii

How to use this book   iv

Chapter 1: Introduction to writing

    1.1 Nouns   1
    1.2 Determiners   4
    1.3 Basic present tenses   5
    1.4 Simple sentence structure   6
    1.5 Subject/verb agreement   8
    1.6 Prepositions   11
    1.7 There is / there are   14
    1.8 Adverbs   15
    1.9 Articles   17
    1.10 Adjectives   21
    1.11 Compare/contrast structures   25
    1.12 Common errors with word forms   27
    1.13 Compound and complex sentence structures   29
    1.14 Transitions   32
    1.15 Sentence fragments and run-on sentences   33
    1.16 Common errors   38
    1.17 Grammar check 1   39
    1.18 Writing practice   40

Chapter 2: Past and present

    2.1 Basic past and present tenses   41
    2.2 Past perfect   44
    2.3 Articles, continued   47
    2.4 Adjective clauses   48
    2.5 Punctuating adjective clauses   53
    2.6 Adjective clause error correction   55
    2.7 Noun clauses   56
    2.8 Reported speech   58
    2.9 Sentence structure: review   61
    2.10 Paragraph development   62
    2.11 Narrative paragraphs   64
    2.12 Grammar check 2   66
    2.13 Writing practice   67

Chapter 3: Introduction to essays

3.1	Introductions	**69**
3.2	Body paragraphs	**70**
3.3	Counter-arguments	**71**
3.4	Conclusions	**73**
3.5	Essay structure: review	**74**
3.6	Putting theory into practice	**75**
3.7	Example argumentative essay: life lessons	**82**
3.8	Parallel structure	**86**
3.9	Passive voice	**88**
3.10	Modal verbs	**91**
3.11	Avoiding weak connections	**96**
3.12	Using personal support	**97**
3.13	Logical fallacies	**98**
3.14	Grammar check 3	**103**
3.15	Writing practice	**104**
3.16	Essay outline	**105**
3.17	Essay checklist	**107**

Chapter 4: Using evidence

4.1	Discursive (compare/contrast) essays	**108**
4.2	Present perfect	**112**
4.3	Gerunds and infinitives	**118**
4.4	Using evidence	**122**
4.5	Citations and references	**123**
4.6	Facts and opinions	**124**
4.7	How to cite and reference	**125**
4.8	Reporting phrases for paraphrasing and quoting	**128**
4.9	Model essay	**129**
4.10	Using evidence: practice 1	**133**
4.11	Using evidence: practice 2	**137**
4.12	Using evidence: practice 3	**139**
4.13	Source analysis	**142**
4.14	Grammar check 4	**144**
4.15	Writing practice	**146**
4.16	Essay outline	**148**
4.17	Essay checklist	**150**

Introduction

Welcome to *Get it Write!*

This book teaches essential grammar and content-development skills in a logical way, enabling intermediate-level students to learn through structured practice exercises and increasingly advanced styles of academic writing.

Progressing gradually from words and sentences through to essays and research writing, *Get it Write!* reviews important aspects of English (such as countable and uncountable nouns, verb tenses, sentence structure and other essential grammar) and research writing (such as incorporating evidence into academic essays using APA citations and references).

Key features:

- Essential grammar and sentence structures, explained and modelled
- 65+ progressive practice exercises, targeting key language and academic writing conventions
- Interesting articles and essay texts
- How to avoid common errors
- How to apply citation and referencing style
- End-of-chapter grammar- and writing-review tasks
- Digital resources, including tests, planning templates and answers

Over the ten years that it has taken to write and refine this book, thousands of students and many teachers have used the materials, and I would like to express my deepest gratitude to all who have helped with its development.

Leigh Pearson, 2023

Leigh Pearson is an experienced teacher of English for Academic Purposes (EAP), and has published many student- and teacher-focused materials throughout his long career. He is a former IELTS Speaking and Writing examiner, and is currently an instructor and level co-ordinator at Mahidol University International College, Thailand.

How to use this book

Get It Write! offers a progression through an intermediate level of English writing, starting with a review of the basics and some of the common mistakes that students make, followed by an increasingly challenging selection of content, grammar, and academic conventions as students learn how to structure, develop, and support academic essays.

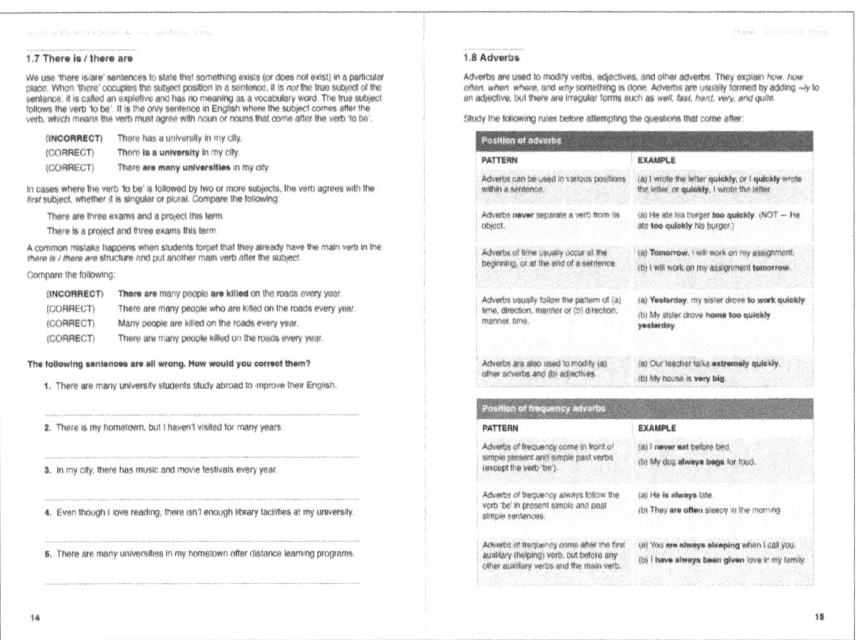

Once students have understood the different grammar and writing conventions presented, they are given structured exercises in which to practice and build their confidence with increasingly more challenging language and development. Each chapter ends with a selection of topics that provide students with an opportunity to reinforce their learning.

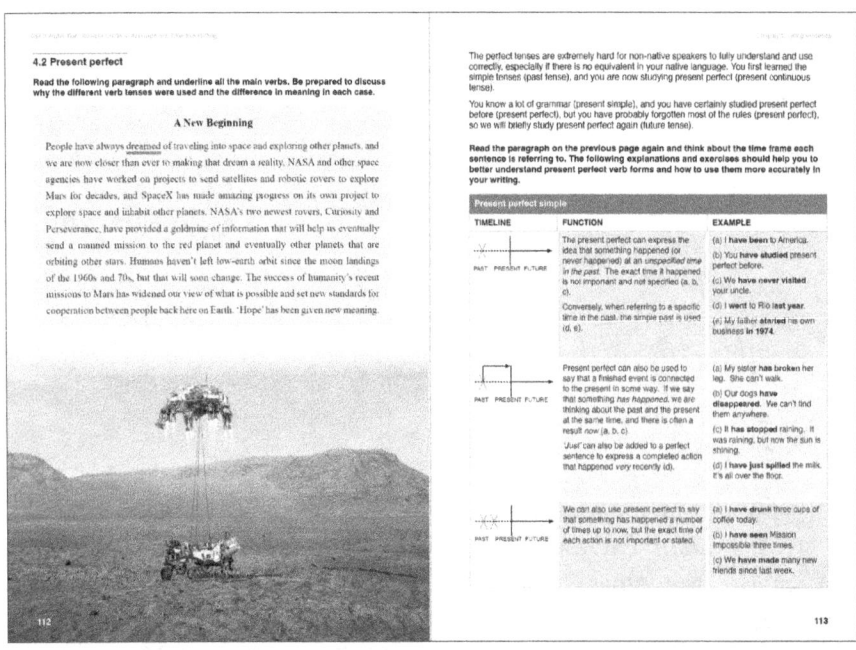

By working through the resource, students learn the rules and conventions of grammar and content development through carefully written descriptions and explanations combined with examples of correct and incorrect language, tables, and model paragraphs and essays.

Chapter 1: Introduction to writing covers countable and uncountable nouns, basic present tenses, sentence structure, and grammar that is useful and appropriate for writing descriptive paragraphs, including articles, preposition phrases, adjectives, and adverbs.

Chapter 2: Past and present progresses into past tenses within the context of narrative paragraphs (stories), ideal for introducing and practicing grammar and more advanced structures such as reported speech, adjective clauses, and noun clauses.

Chapter 3: Introduction to essays introduces basic essay structure and development, including introductions, body paragraphs, counter-arguments and conclusions, and covers useful grammar (such as passive voice and modal verbs) and some of the errors that students commonly make when qualifying statements and logically supporting their ideas.

Chapter 4: Using evidence focuses on research writing and using published evidence to support students' own ideas within an essay, specifically paraphrasing, quoting, and correctly citing and referencing sources using APA conventions; and covers useful grammar such as present perfect tenses, gerunds, and infinitives.

This table identifies the students who will benefit most from *Get It Write!*

IELTS	TOEFL iBT	TOEFL PBT	Cambridge BULATS	TOEIC	CEFR
9	118–120	645–677		950–990	C2
8	110–117	610–644	85–90	900–949	C2
7.5	102–109	581–609	80–85	840–899	C2
7	94–101	560–580	80	780–839	C1
6.5	79–93	546–559	75	735–779	C1
6	60–78	530–545	70	685–734	B2
5.5	42–59	516–529	65	600–684	B2
5	35–41	490–510	60	550–559	B1
4.5	32–34	450–489	50	450–549	B1
4	0–31	400–449	40	200–449	A2
3	0–31	400–449	30	200–449	A2
2					A1

The table is for illustrative purposes only, and there may be differences between institutes and organizations.

Answers and downloadable resources:

To access the accompanying supporting materials and comprehensive answers to all exercises, please visit:

 prosperityeducation.net/get-it-write

- Use the password **TIAB** to access this page.
- Click on the links to download the material.

1. Introduction to writing

1.1 Nouns

Let's begin with the foundation of any sentence — the noun. Every sentence has at least one noun as the subject of the sentence, but if you get the noun wrong, it can cause a chain reaction of errors throughout your writing.

The difficulty comes from the fact that English has countable and uncountable nouns. As an intermediate-level student, you should already be familiar with the basic concept of countable and uncountable nouns, but some nouns can be both countable and uncountable with a slight difference in meaning. This fact causes many problems for English language learners.

An uncountable noun usually refers to something that is hard or impossible to count for some reason. For example, 'tree' is a countable noun, but 'wood' is uncountable because it is a material that can be any size, from a tiny splinter of wood all the way up to a huge log of wood. Similarly, 'fruit' is an uncountable noun that refers to a type of food that grows on a tree or bush, but there are many types of fruit, so all together they are uncountable because there are just so many types. Because we cannot count these nouns, we cannot use numbers with them, and they cannot usually be plural or take the articles a/an.

The following table breaks uncountable nouns into ten categories to make them easier to remember.

Try to memorize all ten categories.

Category	Examples
1. Things that come in very small (hard-to-count) pieces	rice, salt, sand, dirt, hair, flour, dust
2. A group of similar things	food, furniture, luggage, garbage, equipment, money
3. Academic subjects	English, biology, mathematics, economics
4. Abstract ideas	happiness, research, wisdom, news, knowledge
5. Liquids/semi-solids	blood, milk, water, beer, honey, butter
6. Gases	carbon monoxide, oxygen
7. Solids/materials	cheese, gold, ice, plastic, wood, bread
8. Sports/types of recreation	chess, tennis, soccer, jogging, hiking, swimming
9. Natural phenomena	weather, rain, snow, lightning
10. Diseases	cancer, measles, smallpox, Covid-19

Note: To express a specific quantity, some uncountable nouns may be preceded by a unit of measurement such as *a sheet of* paper, *a spoonful of* coffee, and *a piece of* wood.

GET IT WRITE! *The Ultimate Guide to Academic Writing*

You should already be familiar with basic countable and uncountable nouns. However, some nouns have both countable and uncountable forms, with a difference in meaning. These nouns are used to make a distinction between more 'general' and more 'specific' meanings. Common examples include business, time, responsibility, technology, experience, education, school, university, society, and life, to name just a few. Compare the following:

> She has enough **experience** to write a good essay. (experience **in general**)
>
> She had **a** bad **experience** in her exam yesterday. (a **specific** experience)
>
> If I have **time**, I will go on holiday this Christmas. (time **in general**)
>
> We had **a** great **time** at the beach last week. (a **specific** time)

Finally, nouns can sometimes be used as modifiers, similar to how you use adjectives, to modify other nouns, creating a compound noun. For example, a shop that sells makeup is a beauty shop, not a beautiful shop. The first noun 'beauty' is being used an adjective to describe what type of shop it is, not the quality of the shop. Note that when a noun is used as an adjective in this way to modify and describe another noun, it is almost always used in its singular form with no 's'.

> A shop that sells shoes is a **shoe shop** (NOT a shoe**s** shop).
>
> A bag that you use to carry books is **a book bag** (NOT a book**s** bag).

Complete the following sentences with the given word in the correct form to make a grammatically correct sentence. In the parentheses at the end of each sentence, indicate if the noun used is a singular countable noun (SCN), a plural countable noun (PCN), an uncountable noun (UN), or an adjective use of the noun (ADJ). The first one has been done for you as an example. Be prepared to discuss your answers.

1. My city has too many (*vehicle*) __vehicles__ because of the large population. (PCN)
2. His theory is supported by a significant amount of (*research*) _____. ( )
3. Bones and DNA show that all (*human*) _____ evolved in Africa. ( )
4. There are a lot of good (*job*) _____ opportunities in capital cities. ( )
5. The (*evidence*) _____ for climate change should convince anyone. ( )
6. Nobody likes it when they are given (*homework*) _____ every night. ( )
7. Studying in England was the best (*experience*) _____ of my life. ( )
8. Using different (*sentence*) _____ structures is essential to write well. ( )
9. Some (*economy*) _____ will take years to recover from Covid-19. ( )
10. The internet has a lot of useful (*information*) _____. ( )
11. (*News*) _____ stories help us to keep up to date with the world. ( )
12. Every (*child*) _____ should receive healthcare and an education. ( )
13. The computer is one of the most important (*technology*) _____. ( )

Chapter 1: Introduction to writing

As previously mentioned, many nouns have both countable and uncountable forms, with a difference in meaning between more 'general' and more 'specific'.

Complete the following sentences with the given word in the correct form (noun, verb, adjective, adverb) to make each sentence grammatically correct.

1. **(LIFE)** _____ can be very cruel. Every _____ is important, but every day, thousands of _____ are lost in terrible accidents and wars. In order to _____ peacefully and enjoy a good quality of _____, we must try harder to work together.

2. **(SOCIETY)** Every _____ has its own problems. This is partly because people have different _____ values, and people tend to _____ with people who share similar beliefs. Also, a lot of _____ still experience corruption and do not protect their citizens as they should.

3. **(UNIVERSITY)** Going to _____ can be a life-changing experience, and most _____ students go on to build successful careers in the future. There are thousands of great _____ in the world, but choosing a good _____ can be difficult.

4. **(EXPERIENCE)** My trip to the North Pole was one of the most amazing _____ of my life. Over the years, I have gained a lot of _____ with travelling to new places, but that trip was the greatest _____ because I _____ so many extremely difficult but very rewarding situations.

5. **(SUCCESS)** My brother's business is a _____, but it took him many years to _____. Now that he is _____, however, I'm very proud of him. _____ can be very rewarding, but it is rarely easy. Most people _____ through a lot of hard work and determination.

6. **(TECHNOLOGY)** The modern world is full of _____. The wheel is one of the most ubiquitous and important _____ of all time, but information _____ is one of the most recent _____ advances that may eventually lead to true artificial intelligence, or AI.

1.2 Determiners

With nouns, it is often necessary to use a word called a determiner to indicate which thing(s) you are referring to, or whether you are referring to one thing or several. There are two main types of determiners.

Type A determiners are used to say which thing(s) you are referring to and whether you are thinking of a specific example or speaking in general.

> **articles**: a/an/the (we will discuss articles in greater detail later in the book)
>
> **possessives**: my, your, his, their, etc.
>
> **demonstratives**: this, that, these, those

Type B determiners are usually quantifiers that say how much or how many, such as three, some, every, many, all. Some Type B determiners are only used with countable nouns (e.g. every, many, and a few), some are only used with uncountable nouns (e.g. a little), and some can be used with both countable and uncountable (e.g. a lot of and some).

However, if you want to use a Type B determiner (describing how much or how many) before a noun that has a Type A determiner (the, her, this, etc.), you have to use 'of'.

Compare the following:

> **Most** people don't like homework. (CORRECT — people in general)
>
> **Most of** people don't like homework. (**INCORRECT**)
>
> **Most of the** people **in this class** like homework. (CORRECT — a specific group of people)

It's also worth noting here that 'few' and 'a few' (used with countable nouns), and 'little' and 'a little' (used with uncountable nouns) have slightly different meanings. 'Few' and 'little' are more negative and mean 'not many/not much'. Similarly, 'a few' and 'a little' also refer to a relatively small quantity of something, but they are slightly more positive and mean 'some'.

For example, 'I have a few friends' means that I have maybe ten close friends, whereas 'I have few friends' might mean that I have just two or three.

Please also note that a lot of and lots of have the same meaning and can be followed by both countable and uncountable nouns, but they can't be mixed up, i.e. you cannot write there are a lots of people. You must say there are lots of people or there are a lot of people.

Complete the following sentences with 'of' if necessary.

1. Most _____ people enjoy watching movies.

2. I have read a few _____ the books in our library.

3. Many _____ books are available in paperback or hardback.

4. Most _____ our teachers like to give us too much homework.

5. Some _____ the workers at my father's company have quit.

1.3 Basic present tenses

Now that we have covered noun structures, we need a verb to construct a basic sentence. A verb is a word that is used to say what someone or something does or what happens to them, or it can be used as a linking verb followed by an adjective to give information about the subject. You should already be familiar with the basic principles of verbs, but the following explanations and exercises should help you to better understand the basic present tense verb forms and how to use them more accurately in your writing.

The simple tenses		
TIMELINE	**FUNCTION**	**EXAMPLE**
Present Simple XXXXXXX PAST PRESENT FUTURE	Generally, present simple describes permanent situations or things that happen regularly or all the time. A present simple statement was true in the past, is still true now, and will probably be true in the future.	(a) Tom **lives** in New York. (b) It **rains** a lot in England.
Present Progressive PAST PRESENT FUTURE	We use present progressive to talk about: (a) a relatively short-term action that started in the past, is still happening now, and will probably continue in the near future; (b) a development or change in a general situation over a longer period of time.	(a) Jane **is sleeping** at the moment. (b) People **are smoking** less than they did fifty years ago.

Complete the following sentences using either present simple or present continuous.

1. Because it (*rain*) _____, I will stay home and watch TV.

2. The UK is a very green country because it (*rain*) _____ often.

3. I (*work*) _____ on my assignment right now, so I don't have time to eat.

4. My father (*work*) _____ at a bank, but he (*work*) _____ more hours than usual at the moment because he (*save*) _____ money for a new car.

5. People (*have*) _____ fewer children and (*live*) _____ longer than they used to. All economies (*need*) _____ young workers to replace older workers, so many governments (*look*) _____ for solutions to this issue.

1.4 Simple sentence structure

A sentence is a group of words that express a complete idea. A simple sentence contains at least one subject/verb combination. The subject shows who or what does something, and the verb shows the action (or condition). Study the following examples of simple sentences:

Subject(s)	Verb(s)	Pattern
(a) I	study	SV
(b) I	study and work	SVV
(c) I	study, work, and have fun	SVVV
(d) My neck	hurts	SV
(e) You and I	are reading	SSV
(f) My legs, neck, and back	hurt	SSSV
(g)	Work hard!	V

The simplest sentence has one subject and one verb as in (a) and (d) above. However, the verb of a sentence may be compound as in (b) and (c).

Also, the subject of a sentence may be compound as in (e) and (f). Note the use of commas in a list of three or more verbs or nouns, as in (c) and (f). Also, an imperative sentence (an instruction) as in (g) is also a complete sentence as the subject is understood to be 'you', but it is not written.

As well as the subject(s) and verb(s) of your sentence, you may wish to add additional information such as who, what, when, where, why, or how something happens.
The information that comes after the main verb is the called the complement of a sentence. The complement adds meaning to the verb or gives extra information to the sentence.
A sentence can have one of six possible complements.

Study and try to remember the following:

Subject	Verb	Complement
We	like	hotdogs / big juicy hotdogs. (**1. Noun / noun phrase**)
I	understand	you. (**2. Pronoun**)
They	are reading	quietly / very quietly. (**3. Adverb / adverb phrase**)
You	are	smart / very smart. (**4. Adjective / adjective phrase**)*
She	wants	to expand her business. (**5. Verb phrase**)
You	are studying	with new friends. (**6. Prepositional phrase**)

*adjective complements are only possible with a linking verb such as be, look, seem, etc.
For example, she is beautiful; she looks beautiful; she seems beautiful.

A complement can also be a combination of any of the six possible complements.

Subject	Verb	Complement combinations
I	like	exercising. (**gerund noun**)
I	like	exercising in the evening. (**gerund noun + adverb/prep phrase**)
I	like	exercising in the evening with my girlfriend. (**gerund noun + adverb/prep phrase + prepositional phrase**)
I	like	exercising in the evening with my girlfriend to stay fit and healthy. (**gerund noun + adverb/prep phrase + prepositional phrase + verb phrase**)

In the following simple sentences, underline the subjects, double-underline the main verbs, and label all preposition phrases and other 'chunks' of grammar that you can see. The first one has been done for you.

1. The main reason (to learn English) [verb phrase] is (to communicate) [verb phrase] (with foreigners) [prep. phrase].

2. The happiest moment of my life was marrying my wife on a beach in Thailand.

3. It is important to dress appropriately at formal events.

4. In the evenings, my wife and I enjoy watching TV and eating snacks together.

5. During vacations, I usually relax and enjoy my time off with family and friends.

1.5 Subject/verb agreement

You should already be familiar with the basic idea that the subject and verb of a sentence must agree (I, we, you, they **like** / He, she, it **likes**).

My mother *is* American.	(**singular subject + singular verb**)
We *are* students.	(**plural subject + plural verb**)
You and I *work* hard.	(**compound subject + plural verb**)
Swimming *is* good exercise.	(**singular subject** (gerund) **+ singular verb**)

Each and every

One point that often causes confusion is the use of *each* and *every*. *Each* and *every* are always followed immediately by a singular noun, and therefore, the verb must also be singular. In addition, even when there are two or more nouns connected by *and*, the verb remains singular. This rule is also true for *any* as long as it is part of a singular noun such as *anyone* and *anything*, but not if it is used as a determiner; such as *any* books or *any* pens.

Everyone ***dreams***.

Every child ***needs*** love.

Every glass, cup, and plate *is* broken.

Prepositional phrases

The subject of a sentence is often preceded or followed by a prepositional phrase, which can make choosing the right verb difficult. A prepositional phrase is a group of words that starts with a preposition and ends with a noun, pronoun, or noun phrase. Prepositional phrases express where, when, how, why, or whose. Pay particular attention to the last column!

near New York	**on** January 3rd	**due to** the rain
by bus	**of** my books	**despite** the time
in the corner	**by** writing carefully	**as a result of** my boss
among friends	**without** warning	**during** the movie

When a prepositional phrase comes after the subject of a sentence, it is important to remember that it is *not a part of* the subject. You should therefore ignore it most of the time when you are deciding which verb to use.

That bag (of books) *is* very heavy.

His interest (in so many subjects) *takes* a lot of his free time.

The assignments (from our teacher) *are* very interesting.

If a sentence *starts* with a prepositional phrase of time or place, there is a comma separating it from the subject. Remember that a prepositional phrase **cannot** be the subject of a sentence!

(**INCORRECT**) *In my school* has very kind teachers.
(CORRECT) *In my school,* the teachers are very kind.

Quantifiers as subjects

Another area of confusion occurs when a quantifier is used as the subject of a sentence.

One of my teeth *is* missing, and **both** of my children *are laughing* at me.

Here, the first subject is *one*, which is always singular, and the second subject is *both*, which is always plural. Notice that '*one of*' is always followed by a plural noun (one of many).

Here are some more examples of singular and plural subjects.

Singular subjects

Neither (of my parents) *is* living. They both died when I was young.

Much (of their time) *is* spent doing homework.

Either (of your books) *explains* verb tenses very well.

Plural subjects

Both (of my parents) *were* very kind.

Several (of the teachers) *are* very cruel.

Many (people) still *don't believe* in climate change

A few (students) *love* grammar!

Unfortunately, the difference between singular and plural subjects is not always clear. Some quantifiers can be both singular *and* plural.

In these cases, you must look at the noun in the prepositional phrase to see whether your verb should be singular or plural.

None (of the **jewelry**) *is* expensive.	(uncountable — **singular**)
None (of the **diamonds**) *are* real.	(countable — **plural**)
Some (of my **money**) *was* stolen.	(uncountable — **singular**)
Some (of his **books**) *are* in my car.	(countable — **plural**)
A lot (of our **homework**) *is* very difficult.	(uncountable — **singular**)
A lot (of **textbooks**) *are* very complicated.	(countable — **plural**)
Most (of the **pollution**) *comes* from cars.	(uncountable — **singular**)
Most (of my **friends**) *have* part-time jobs.	(countable — **plural**)
All (of the **ice**) *has melted*.	(uncountable — **singular**)
All (of their **phones**) *are* better than mine.	(countable — **plural**)

GET IT WRITE! *The Ultimate Guide to Academic Writing*

Complete the following sentences using an appropriate form of the verb in parentheses. Be careful of tenses in some cases. To help you complete this task, underline or highlight the subject of each sentence and put parentheses around any preposition phrases.

1. Every boss and employee (*know*) _____ the importance of teamwork.

2. Writing paragraphs (*help*) _____ a reader to understand your ideas.

3. My mother and father (*move*) _____ to a new house at the moment.

4. The ideas in the lecture (*help*) _____ you pass the exam next week.

5. The teachers at my old school (*be*) _____ always kind to me.

6. One of my teachers and two of my friends (*come*) _____ from England.

7. Most of the fun during holidays (*happen*) _____ at night.

8. The wildlife in zoos (*help*) _____ us to understand the natural world.

9. There (*be*) _____ a lot of TOEFL and IELTS resources available online.

10. Most pollution in rivers (*be*) _____ caused by people.

11. Everybody in my class (*love*) _____ doing homework every night.

12. One of the best things in my life at the moment (*be*) _____ my beautiful new child.

13. Each explanation and exercise in these chapters (*improve*) _____ your English.

14. All of the dirty black smoke from cars and buses on the streets of all big cities (*damage*) _____ our health and the environment.

15. Having loving relationships in today's busy world with so many responsibilities (*be*) _____ very important, but it can (*be*) _____ difficult.

1.6 Prepositions

Earlier in Chapter 1, we briefly discussed prepositional phrases. Now we will cover prepositions when they are used after a verb or adjective. Often, the correct preposition cannot be guessed, and one has to learn and remember each expression as a whole.

The fact that there are so many prepositions and you have to remember each one individually means that prepositions will probably continue to cause errors in your writing far into the future, but a few important rules for using prepositions are as follows:

~ing forms used as nouns

When we put a verb after a preposition, we usually use an ~ing form (a gerund), not an infinitive. Compare the following:

>You can't improve your writing **without practicing**.
>
>You can pass the exam **by studying** hard.
>
>My friends are talking **about playing** football after class.
>
>She fell asleep **after watching** TV all night.
>
>**Before going** to bed, I always read a book.

'To' as a preposition

'To' actually has two different uses. It can be used to indicate that the next word is an infinitive verb (e.g. **to** write, **to** read), or it can be used as a preposition before a noun, pronoun, or noun phrase (e.g. He's gone **to** school. I always listen **to** my parents).

Study the following examples and discuss the differences:

>**I like to learn about science.** (*learn* is a verb, so *to learn* is an infinitive verb)
>
>**I went to a cool science festival last month.** (*a cool science festival* is a noun phrase, so *to a cool science festival* is a preposition phrase)
>
>**In class, you must stick to the rules.** (*the rules* is a noun, so *to the rules* is a preposition phrase)
>
>**I get to college by bus.** (*college* is a noun, so *to college* is a preposition phrase)
>
>**I hope to graduate next year.** (*graduate* is a verb, so *to graduate* is an infinitive verb)
>
>**It is important to brainstorm and plan your essays first.** (*brainstorm* and *plan* are both verbs in this sentence, so *to brainstorm and plan* is actually two infinitive verbs, but we only need to include a single *to*. We could say *It is important to brainstorm and to plan your essays first*, but the second *to* is unnecessary.)

Complete the following sentences with appropriate prepositions *if one is necessary*. These sentences contain some very common preposition mistakes that we see in student writing, so don't assume you know the correct answer.

Think carefully, and be careful as some of these sentences do not require any preposition at all!

1. I want to be good _____ English.

2. The girl over there reminds me _____ my sister.

3. I am looking forward _____ meeting you next week.

4. For my degree, I want to study _____ international business _____ university.

5. My wife and I discussed _____ having a baby last night.

6. As a university student, you can access _____ a lot of information and services.

7. In last week's classes, our teacher explained simple sentences _____ us.

8. Winter is great because you can throw snowballs _____ everyone.

9. Last night, I was driving too fast and crashed _____ a wall.

10. In my house, I am responsible _____ cooking and looking after our pets.

11. Drugs and alcohol can have a big effect _____ people's performance.

12. When you enter _____ college, you will face _____ a lot of obstacles.

13. Every weekend, my parents try _____ prevent me _____ going out.

14. I apologized _____ my girlfriend _____ making her cry.

15. Many people use the internet _____ search _____ information.

The following table lists a few common verb/adjective + preposition combinations.

Verb/adjective + preposition combinations	
absent from something	kind to somebody
accuse somebody of doing something.	laugh at somebody or something
agree with a person or idea	made of/from a material
anxious about (= worried about)	made by somebody
apply to somewhere for something	made with a tool
bad at	near (to) somebody or something
believe in God, ghosts etc	pay for something
blame somebody for something	pleased with somebody/something
care about something (= important)	pray for something
take care of (= look after)	prevent somebody or something from doing something (= stop something before it happens)
care for (= look after or like)	
crash into something	
depend on somebody or something for something	protect somebody or something from danger of some kind
	recover from an illness
disappointed with somebody or something for something	rely on somebody or something
	remind somebody of something
divide into	remind somebody to do something (= make them remember to do something they might forget)
dream of (= think of, imagine)	
dream about (while asleep)	
fight with somebody or a situation	responsible for
fight for something one believes in	search for somebody or something
forgive somebody for something	surprised by something
get in (to) and out of a car	study for an exam or qualification
get on (to) and off a motorbike, plane, train, bus, or ship	study a subject (no preposition)
	take part in an activity
good at	talk to somebody about something
graduate from a university	throw something at (= throw to hit)
graduate in a subject	throw something to (= throw to be caught)
graduated with a qualification	used to something (= accustomed to)
insist on something	

1.7 There is / there are

We use 'there is/are' sentences to state that something exists (or does not exist) in a particular place. When 'there' occupies the subject position in a sentence, it is *not* the true subject of the sentence; it is called an expletive and has no meaning as a vocabulary word. The true subject follows the verb 'to be'. It is the only sentence in English where the subject comes after the verb, which means the verb must agree with noun or nouns that come after the verb 'to be'.

(**INCORRECT**)	There has a university in my city.
(CORRECT)	There **is a university** in my city.
(CORRECT)	There **are many universities** in my city.

In cases where the verb 'to be' is followed by two or more subjects, the verb agrees with the *first* subject, whether it is singular or plural. Compare the following:

There are three exams and a project this term.

There is a project and three exams this term.

A common mistake happens when students forget that they already have the main verb in the *there is / there are* structure and put another main verb after the subject.

Compare the following:

(**INCORRECT**)	**There are** many people **are killed** on the roads every year.
(CORRECT)	There are many people who are killed on the roads every year.
(CORRECT)	Many people are killed on the roads every year.
(CORRECT)	There are many people killed on the roads every year.

The following sentences are all wrong. How would you correct them?

1. There are many university students study abroad to improve their English.

   _____

2. There is my hometown, but I haven't visited for many years.

   _____

3. In my city, there has music and movie festivals every year.

   _____

4. Even though I love reading, there isn't enough library facilities at my university.

   _____

5. There are many universities in my hometown offer distance learning programs.

   _____

1.8 Adverbs

Adverbs are used to modify verbs, adjectives, and other adverbs. They explain *how, how often, when, where,* and *why* something is done. Adverbs are usually formed by adding *~ly* to an adjective, but there are irregular forms such as *well, fast, hard, very, and quite*.

Study the following rules before attempting the questions that come after:

Position of adverbs

PATTERN	EXAMPLE
Adverbs can be used in various positions within a sentence.	(a) I wrote the letter **quickly,** or I **quickly** wrote the letter, or **quickly**, I wrote the letter.
Adverbs **never** separate a verb from its object.	(a) He ate his burger **too quickly**. (NOT — He ate **too quickly** his burger.)
Adverbs of time usually occur at the beginning, or at the end of a sentence.	(a) **Tomorrow**, I will work on my assignment. (b) I will work on my assignment **tomorrow**.
Adverbs usually follow the pattern of (a) time, direction, manner or (b) direction, manner, time.	(a) **Yesterday**, my sister drove **to work quickly**. (b) My sister drove **home too quickly yesterday**.
Adverbs are also used to modify (a) other adverbs and (b) adjectives.	(a) Our teacher talks **extremely quickly**. (b) My house is **very big**.

Position of frequency adverbs

PATTERN	EXAMPLE
Adverbs of frequency come in front of simple present and simple past verbs (except the verb 'be').	(a) I **never eat** before bed. (b) My dog **always begs** for food.
Adverbs of frequency always follow the verb 'be' in present simple and past simple sentences.	(a) He **is always** late. (b) They **are often** sleepy in the morning.
Adverbs of frequency come after the first auxiliary (helping) verb, but before any other auxiliary verbs and the main verb.	(a) You **are always sleeping** when I call you. (b) I **have always been given** love in my family.

Put all of the following words together to form grammatically correct sentences. As you complete this exercise, think carefully about which words are adverbs, what these words are describing, and where they must appear within each sentence.

1. work / of / every day / most / friends / diligently / my / very

   _____

2. his / safely / night / John / car / usually / drives / very / at / home

   _____

3. escapes / fence / one / often / dogs / over / night / the / of / at / my

   _____

4. brother / talk / my / doesn't / quietly / always / very

   _____

Choose whether to use the adjective or adverb to complete the following sentences. Think carefully about the sentence structure and decide whether the missing word is describing a noun, verb, adjective, or adverb. If the missing word is describing a noun, you need to use an adjective. On the other hand, if the missing word is describing a verb, adjective, or adverb, then you need to use an adverb.

1. The (*guilty / guiltily*) _____ but (*shameless / shamelessly*) _____ ex-president walked (*slow / slowly*) _____ towards his new prison cell.

2. Students can (*easy / easily*) _____ access the library on campus, but they must remain (*quiet / quietly*) _____ at all times so that they do not disturb others.

3. It is important to behave (*responsible / responsibly*) _____ in life because if you are (*unreliable / unreliably*) _____, people will not trust you.

4. Information is (*easy / easily*) _____ to access these days because the internet is (*quick / quickly*) _____, and global access is increasing.

5. Oil prices have increased (*significant / significantly*) _____ in recent years, so there has also been an (*extreme / extremely*) _____ concerning drop in demand.

1.9 Articles

Articles are one of the hardest aspects of English grammar to get right because there are so many rules to remember. The following tables explain all the rules for the articles *a*, *an*, *the*, *no article*, *some*, and *any*. Study these rules very carefully before you attempt the questions after:

A/an		
The original meaning of a/an was 'one', so it is mainly used with singular countable nouns. *A/an* is generally used as an *indefinite* determiner to show that you are referring to a non-specific thing, or a thing that is not known by the reader.		
	FUNCTION	**EXAMPLE**
Which one	*A/an* can be used with a singular countable noun to talk about a person or thing when the reader does not know which one is being referred to, or when it does not matter which one.	(a) I need **a pen**. (b) We saw **a snake** yesterday. (c) My father is buying **a new car**.
One of many	*A/an* can be used with singular countable nouns to talk about something in general; in (a) the writer is talking about any single pen, but not a specific pen.	(a) **A pen** is a very useful tool. (b) **A snake** is a dangerous animal. (c) Good writers use **a dictionary**.
Description	*A/an* can be used after a linking verb such as *be* and *become* to show that person or thing belongs to a class, group, or type.	(a) My brother is **a plumber**. (b) I miss being **a student**.

Would you like an apple?

The

The can be used with singular, plural, and uncountable nouns. *The* is a *definite* determiner; it is used when the reader knows (or can work out) which person(s) or thing(s) you are talking about.

	FUNCTION	**EXAMPLE**
Which one	*The* can be used when it is clear from the situation which one(s) you are discussing.	(a) John's in **the toilet**. (b) Can I borrow **the car** today?
	The can be used when you have mentioned the person(s) or thing(s) before.	(a) I put some money in my wallet, but today, **the money** has gone.
	The can be used when you say in the sentence which one(s) you mean.	(a) **The girl who sits next to me** is very nice. (b) Where is **the money I gave you**?
The only one(s)	*The* can be used when you are talking about something unique such as *the sun* or *the stars*, or when something is unique to our environment such as *the police* or *the government*.	(a) **The Second World War** was terrible. (b) **The prime minister** has helped my country's economy a lot.
Place names	*The* is usually used with *seas, mountain groups, island groups, rivers, deserts, hotels, cinemas, museums, and newspapers*. See ø (no article) for place names without *the*.	(a) **The Pacific Ocean** is huge. (b) **The Thames River** is in London.
Animals, body parts, and inventions	*The* can be used to refer to an entire group of things, but instead of using the plural, we can use *the + singular noun*. However, this structure can only be used with animals, body parts, and inventions.	(a) **The** blue whale is the world's largest mammal. (b) **The** brain is the most complex human organ. (c) **The** computer has revolutionized the way we work.

Chapter 1: Introduction to writing

Ø (no article)

Ø (no article) can only be used with uncountable and plural nouns. It cannot be used with singular nouns. We use no article when to talk about something in general.

	FUNCTION	EXAMPLE
Things in general	No article (Ø) is used when you are talking about something in general;	(a) **Pens** are very useful. (b) I hate **snakes**. (c) **Fruit** is good for your health.
Fixed expressions of place, time, and movement	Some countable nouns are used as uncountable with no article. to/at/from/enter school/university to/at/in/into/from church to/at/from/leave work or home by train/bus/car/bicycle	(a) I will meet you at **university**. (b) My wife is at **home** now.
Proper names	We do not usually use an article with singular proper names	(a) Her name is **Jane**. (b) I love **Manchester United**.
Place names	Ø (no article) is usually used with continents, countries, provinces, towns, streets, lakes, and titles of public buildings or organizations.	(a) **Oxford Street** has a lot of shops. (b) **Central Park** is a beautiful place to relax.

Some/any

	FUNCTION	EXAMPLE
Quantity	*Some* and *any* are used to express a limited but uncertain quantity — when we do not know, care, or say exactly how much or how many. *Some* is usually used in positive sentences, but *any* is usually used in negative sentences and questions. In (c), *some* is often used in questions when the speaker expects a positive response.	(a) I bought **some fruit**, but I did not buy **any coffee**. (b) Have you got **any children**? (c) Could you lend me **some money**?

19

Complete the following sentences using an appropriate article (a/an/the/some/any) or Ø if no article is required.

1. Our teacher gave us _____ homework last night.

2. _____ homework is always boring!

3. _____ homework that our teacher gave us yesterday was very difficult.

4. I have to clear up all _____ rubbish in my back garden.

5. Too many factories pollute our environment with _____ chemicals.

6. I always try to buy products that don't contain _____ chemicals.

7. Who is _____ man who is sitting next to Jane?

8. We live on _____ Gorky Street, near _____ Waldorf Hotel.

9. My father always wanted to be _____ architect.

10. _____ architect designs buildings.

11. _____ architect who designed my home was terrible! _____ roof leaks whenever it rains, and none of _____ windows close properly.

12. We went to _____ supermarket yesterday and bought _____ fruit and vegetables. We didn't buy _____ meat because we ran out of _____ money. _____ fruit was very fresh, but _____ vegetables were a little bit old, so _____ shop vendor gave us _____ discount.

13. My girlfriend and I have just moved into _____ new house. It's in _____ great location near _____ place where we both work. _____ house has _____ kitchen and _____ bathroom, but there isn't _____ furniture, so we had to buy _____ things to make _____ life more comfortable. We bought _____ bed for our bedroom, and _____ sofa set for _____ living room. _____ sofa set was very expensive because it is made of _____ leather, but it's very comfortable. Once we have finished decorating inside, we will start on _____ garden. At the moment, it looks like _____ jungle, but with _____ lots of hard work we could make it into _____ most beautiful garden in _____ village.

1.10 Adjectives

Adjectives are extremely important in English as they can add much more information and meaning to a sentence. For example, the sentence 'I have a car' doesn't really convey much meaning except ownership. However, the sentence 'I have a terrible old Russian car' tells you much more because of all the adjectives. You should already be familiar with basic adjectives and how to use them, but here are a few rules that you might not be aware of.

Before a noun

When adjectives are used before a noun, they are generally put in the following order:

Adjective order								
Quantity	Opinion	Size	Age	Color	Origin	Material	Purpose	Noun
A	lovely	little	modern	white	English	metal	tea	pot
Three	useless	big	old	brown	French	wooden	fishing	boats

Another point worth noting is that adjectives with **similar** meanings (especially in longer sequences) are generally separated with commas.

A **beautiful**, **expensive**, **luxurious** home.

In cases like this, we might also choose to add 'and' before the last adjective

A **beautiful**, **expensive**, *and* **luxurious** home.

However, shorter, more common adjectives describing different aspects of a noun are usually used without commas.

A **big old African** elephant.

Usually, we do not use 'and' to link adjectives if they are before a noun, but if two adjectives describe the same thing such as character (a) or appearance (b), then 'and' is used.

(a) My **brave** *and* **fearless** dog attacked the thief.

(b) I gave my brother a **red** *and* **yellow** jacket for Christmas.

Finally, we sometimes use two or more words *together* to form a single compound adjective.

I wrote a **250-page** report.

For compound adjectives such as '**250-page**' above, we use a hyphen to join all the words together to form a single adjective because each of the words *alone* would not logically describe the report. For instance, we *cannot* say "I wrote a 250 report", or "I wrote a page report". In addition, any noun that forms part of the compound adjective (such as 'page' in the example above) should be in its singular form without 's'. For example, we *cannot* say "I wrote a 250-page<u>s</u> report".

Finally, with expressions of measurement, the adjective comes after the quantity.

I have a **six-foot-tall** son (*tall* is the adjective of measurement).

I have a **25-meter-long** swimming pool (*long* is the adjective of measurement).

After a noun

When adjectives come after a noun, they must be linked to the noun with a linking verb, such as *be*, *become*, *look*, *seem*, *feel*, *smell*, and *taste*.

　　The teacher **seems/looks/sounds happy** today.

　　The soup **smells/tastes/looks delicious**.

As with adjective before a noun, with expressions of measurement, the adjective comes after the quantity.

　　My son is **six feet tall** (*tall* is the adjective of measurement).

　　My swimming pool is **25 meters long** (*long* is the adjective of measurement).

Finally, we usually use *and* before the last adjective in a series *after* a noun.

　　My girlfriend is tall, slim, **and** beautiful.

Complete the following sentences with the information in parentheses. Look back at the adjective rules on the previous page for guidance.

1. I bought _____ (*computer, new, some, awesome*) games.

2. I love _____ (*old, Chinese, beautiful*) paintings.

3. My dog is _____ (*old, cute, fat*).

4. I own _____ (*black, beautiful, a, white*) cat.

5. I have _____ (*year, 60, old, a, British*) car.

Participle adjectives

This is a **confusing** grammar point that **confuses** many students, but you will not be **confused** for long. The present participle '~ing' is used to show that something has an *active* effect. Think of the 'ing' adjective as describing the quality of something. In this example, the grammar point *confuses* people (*active verb*), so it is a *confusing* grammar point (*adjective*), or this grammar point is/feels/seems *confusing* (*adjective*). On the other hand, everyone is *confused by this grammar point* (*passive verb*), *so* everyone is/feels/seems *confused* (*adjective*). The 'ed' adjectives is used to show the effect *on* something or someone, not the active effect *on something or someone else*. Compare the following examples:

Science **interests** me.

This science book is very **interesting**.

I have been **interested** in science for years.

Grammar **bores** me.

Grammar is very **boring**.

I am **bored**.

Parties **excite** me.

Parties are extremely **exciting**.

I am always **excited** when I go to parties.

Be careful! Not all adjectives have an 'ing' and/or 'ed' form, but in general, the 'ing' adjective describes the quality of something, whereas the 'ed' adjective describes how someone feels (the effect on them).

If we wish to use a comparative form of these adjectives, we have to use 'more' and 'the most'. We cannot use 'er' and 'est'. For example, we might say, "This movie is *more boring* than I expected. In fact, it is *the most boring* movie I have ever seen!"

GET IT WRITE! *The Ultimate Guide to Academic Writing*

Complete the following sentences with participle adjectives from the information in parentheses. Be careful! You might also need to add a linking verb such as is, feel, seem, etc. In addition, you also have to include some adverbs, so refer back to the adverbs section to review how they should be used in a sentence.

For instance, 'John usually feels tired' (adverb of frequency before the main verb) could also be written as 'John is usually tired' (adverb of frequency after the verb 'to be').

1. My friends and I ___are always confused___ (*confuse, always*) by grammar, but when we ask our teacher, it _____ (*usually, confuse, less*).

2. When I got home last night, I noticed that a window _____ (*break*) and the TV and stereo _____ (*miss*).

3. Many students think that reading classes _____ (*bore*), but just because you _____ (*bore*), that does not mean you can fall asleep behind your book!

4. I _____ (*never, relax*) during journeys on public transport in the past, but now that I have a car, journeys _____ (*relax, more*).

5. Exam results _____ (*excite, always*) and _____ (*frighten*) because everyone _____ (*frighten*) of failing.

6. After an _____ (*exhaust*) day at work, I _____ (*always, tire*) and need to sleep early.

7. I have _____ (*extremely, interest*) in science since I was young. Every week, there _____ (*new, amaze*) discoveries about our world!

8. I have an _____ (*interest*) job and a _____ (*love*) wife, so I _____ (*satisfy*) with my life.

9. Many of the stories in the news _____ (*concern, very*). We should all _____ (*concern*) about what our leaders are doing.

10. Living in my local area can _____ (*stress, quite*) because many young people _____ (*addict*) to drugs, so it is not safe at night.

1.11 Compare/contrast structures

A common technique in any language is to compare or contrast two or more things in order to explain how they are similar or how they differ. There are a few comparative structures in the following table that you can use, starting with the easiest and progressing to structures that often cause problems in student writing.

Compare/contrast		
FUNCTION	**STRUCTURE**	**EXAMPLE**
Comparative adjectives	We use comparative adjectives to contrast one thing with another. One-syllable adjectives usually have comparatives ending in ~er, as in (a). Adjectives ending in ~y have ~ier, as in (b). Adjectives with one vowel and one consonant end with *double consonant + ~er*, as in (c). Longer adjectives of two syllables or more usually have *more…*, as in (d).	(a) I am **older** than my brother. (b) He is **luckier** than me. (c) I am not **thin**, but I am **thinner** than him. (d) He is **more handsome** than me.
Superlative adjectives	We use superlative adjectives to compare somebody or something with the group that they belong to. Superlative adjectives are usually preceded by *the*. One-syllable adjectives usually have superlatives ending in ~est, as in (a). Adjectives ending in ~y have ~iest, as in (b). Adjectives with one vowel and one consonant end with *double consonant + ~est*, as in (c). Longer adjectives of two syllables or more usually have *the most…*, as in (d).	(a) I am **the oldest** of four brothers. (b) He is **the luckiest** person in our family. (c) She is **the thinnest** person I have ever seen. (d) That is **the most amazing** car in the showroom.
Similarity	If we want to say that two things are similar, we can use the verb *like*, adverbs such as *too*, *also*, and *as well*, or *the same as* if two things are identical. Note that you can never say *as same as*.	(a) I look **like** my brother. (b) My brother is tall, and I am **too**. (c) My brother is **the same** height **as** me.
Equality	If we want to say that two things are equal in some way, we can use *as adjective as*.	(a) My wife is **as beautiful as** a princess.
Noun structures	If we want to compare or contrast a quantity, we can use the same *as…as* structure, but we use *much + uncountable noun* or *many + plural noun*.	(a) I don't have **as much time as** you. (b) My father doesn't have **as many books as** me.

Choose the best option to complete the following sentences.

1. My house has six bedrooms, but my brother's house only has one.

   My house is (*more big than, more bigger than, bigger than*) my brother's.

2. My friend and I both have five English classes a week.

   We have (*classes as many as, as many classes as, as same classes as*) each other.

3. I have just an hour or two to relax in an evening, but my baby brother can relax all day.

   My brother has (*free time more than me, more free time than me*).

4. I earn a lot of money, but my father earns more than me.

   I don't earn (*money as much as, as much money as, as many money as*) my father.

5. My cousin never does his homework.

   He is (*interested more, more interested, more interesting*) in playing with his friends.

6. It is still hot, but it was hotter yesterday.

   It is not (*hot as same as, as hot as, the same hot as*) yesterday.

7. The price of petrol goes up every year.

   It gets (*expensive more, more expensive, more expensiver*) to drive a car every year.

8. Everyone in my family has blue eyes. My eyes are blue, too.

   My eyes are (*as same color as, the same color as*) everyone else in my family.

9. Everyone thinks that I am a bad driver, but I know that I am a terrible driver.

   When I passed my test, no one was (*surprised the same as, more surprised than, more surprising than*) me!

10. Last night, I went to see a movie, but I fell asleep because the movie was so bad.

    It was (*the most bored, the most boringest, the most boring*) movie I have ever seen.

1.12 Common errors with word forms

We have now covered nouns, verbs, and adjectives, so let's see if you can figure out some of the more common mistakes that learners make with word forms. From the box below, choose the appropriate word for each gap and change it (if necessary) into the appropriate part of speech to form a grammatically correct sentence. Each numbered sentence requires you to use different forms of the same word. The first one has been done for you as an example. To help you do this, think about sentence structure and write n (noun), v (verb), adj (adjective), or adv (adverb) in the parentheses after each word.

~~tell~~	life	death	tiredness	success
responsibility	society	advice	belief	concern

1. My wife always ___tells___ (v) me that she loves me, but yesterday, she ___told___ (v) me that she hated me!

2. Many people don't really enjoy _____ (   ) with others, but they want company at home. This is why many people in _____ (   ) have a fish tank in their homes.

3. In my apartment, I have a small fish tank. I am usually a very _____ (   ) person, so it's my _____ (   ) to clean it every two weeks.

4. However, I am actually quite lazy, and cleaning the tank can be _____ (   ), so I thought of a plan to make my life easier so I wouldn't be so _____ (   ).

5. Last week, I bought a new fish. My plan was to buy a fish that would eat the dirt and keep the tank clean. If my plan was _____ (   ), I would not have to clean the tank anymore. A friend had _____ (   ) by doing the same thing, so I was sure my plan would _____ (   ).

6. I hoped that the new fish would _____ (   ) happily with the one other fish and enjoy its _____ (   ) in my fish tank because there is a lot of dirt for it to eat!

7. Usually, I listen to my wife's _____ (   ), but when I showed her the new fish, she _____ (   ) me not to put it in our fish tank.

8. However, my _____ (   ) that this fish would make my life easier was so strong that I didn't _____ (   ) my wife and put the fish in the tank, anyway.

9. A couple of days ago, I was _____ (   ) when I noticed that the new fish had disappeared. This was very _____ (   ) because the fish was quite big, but after an hour of looking, I still couldn't see it.

10. My new fish is now _____ (   ), which is why my wife is angry with me! I'm not sure exactly when it _____ (   ), but it was my own fault because I put it in the tank with a Siamese fighting fish. Its _____ (   ) is on my shoulders!

1.13 Compound and complex sentence structures

A sentence must have at least one clause (one subject/verb combination that expresses one idea). However, multiple clauses can be combined into a single sentence in order to show how different information relates to each other. Conjunctions must be used to combine two or more clauses together into a single sentence. Conjunctions are used to make two kinds of sentences: Compound sentences and complex sentences.

Compound sentences

Compound sentences are formed using coordinating conjunctions **and**, **or**, **but**, and **so** (**yet**, **for**, and **nor** are also coordinating conjunctions, but are not commonly used these days). These compound conjunctions express different relationships between the two independent clauses.

He studies hard, **and** he always does his homework.	(**ADDITION**)
We drove very quickly, **but** we still arrived late.	(**CONTRAST**)
I went to bed late last night, **so** I feel really sleepy today.	(**RESULT**)
You could go to the cinema, **or** you could just stay at home.	(**CHOICE**)

Independent clauses must be joined with a comma *and* a coordinating conjunction, or separated with a full stop. Compare the following:

(**INCORRECT**)	It was snowing**,** I went skiing.
(CORRECT)	It was snowing**.** I went skiing.
(CORRECT)	It was snowing**,** **so** I went skiing.

In formal writing, coordinating conjunctions cannot be used to start a sentence.

(**INCORRECT**)	My brother was playing a game. **But,** I just watched.
(CORRECT)	My brother was playing a game. I just watched.
(CORRECT)	My brother was playing a game**, but** I just watched.
(CORRECT)	My brother was playing a game. **However,** I just watched.

Although there are exceptions, a comma usually comes after the first clause and before the coordinating conjunction. Notice that the comma comes immediately after the word 'animals' with no space before it.

(**INCORRECT**)	Most people like animals **but** my mother hates them.
(CORRECT)	Most people like animals**, but** my mother hates them.

NOTE: *So that* is often confused with *so*, especially when deciding whether or not to add a comma. *So that* expresses purpose, not result, but *that* is often omitted in less formal writing, which leads to confusion over commas.

Compare the following:

I went out in the rain without an umbrella**, so** I got wet.	(**RESULT**)
Next time, I will take an umbrella **so** (**that**) I will not get wet.	(**REASON**)

Complex sentences

An *independent clause* is a complete sentence and can stand alone. A complex sentence contains an independent clause and another clause joined with a subordinating conjunction. The resulting *dependent clause,* containing the conjunction and the extra clause, cannot stand alone as a sentence; it acts as part of the main clause and *depends* on more information in order to make it a complete sentence.

There are different types of complex sentence, but for the moment we will cover adverb clauses, which use subordinating conjunctions such as *because, although, when,* and *if.*

Study the following example sentences and the table of common subordinating adverbial conjunctions that comes after:

Independent clause	**Dependent clause**
I bought you a special present	because it is your birthday.

Dependent clause	**Independent clause**
Because it is your birthday,	I bought you a special present.

Independent clause	**Dependent clause**
He woke up extremely early	even though it was his day off.

Dependent clause	**Independent clause**
Even though it was his day off,	he woke up extremely early.

Summary of common adverbial conjunctions

Time	Cause/effect	Opposition	Condition
after	because	even though	if
before	since	although	unless
when	now that	though	whether or not
while	as	whereas*	even if
as	as long as	while*	providing (that)
since	so (that)		in case (that)
until			in the event (that)
as soon as			
once			
as long as			
whenever			

*when *while* and *whereas* are used to show opposition, a comma is usually used even if the adverb clause comes second. For example, I hate football, *whereas* my brother loves it.

When a sentence starts with an adverb (dependent) clause, a comma separates the two clauses.

| (**INCORRECT**) | **If you work hard** you will pass. |
| (CORRECT) | **If you work hard,** you will pass. |

Although there are some exceptions, if an adverb (dependent) clause comes *after* an independent clause, there is usually no comma separating the two clauses.

| (**INCORRECT**) | You will pass**, if you work hard**. |
| (CORRECT) | You will pass **if you work hard**. |

One conjunction is enough to join two clauses. Having two conjunctions joining the same main clauses is incorrect.

| (**INCORRECT**) | **Because** it is your birthday, **so** I bought you a present. |
| (CORRECT) | **Because** it is your birthday, I bought you a present. |

Be careful of expressions such as *because of*, *due to*, *in spite of*, *despite* and *during* which are not conjunctions and cannot combine clauses. They are used as prepositions and must therefore be followed by nouns, pronouns, or noun phrases.

Compare the following:

(**INCORRECT**)	We can't play football **because of** it is raining.
(CORRECT)	We can't play football **because** it is raining.
(CORRECT)	We can't play football **because of** the rain.
(CORRECT)	**Because** it is raining, we can't play football.
(CORRECT)	**Because of** the rain, we can't play football.

Compound/Complex sentences

A compound/complex sentence is exactly what it sounds like; it is a sentence that contains three or more clauses joined by two or more coordinating *and* subordinating conjunctions depending on how the clauses relate to each other.

Of course, sentences like this will be longer than a regular compound or complex sentence, so you must be very careful to remember which clauses you are joining with which conjunctions.

Study the following examples and label the subject and verb of each clause and the conjunctions that are joining the clauses together:

> **If** you want to pass the exam, you must work hard in class, **but** you should also work hard in your free time.

> **If** you want to pass the exam, **but** you don't really like studying, you might find it very difficult to pass!

> I don't really enjoy studying, **but** I know that I must get a good GPA **if** I want to get into a good university.

1.14 Transitions

Transitions, such as *in addition, however, moreover, as a result*, etc., serve as a bridge between ideas, but they do not serve as conjunctions to combine clauses into a single sentence. They show the relationship between separate sentences and paragraphs. It is important to remember that they are used to connect ideas, not to connect clauses. They are *not* conjunctions and should *not* be used as such.

(**INCORRECT**)	I work very hard however I still find time to relax.
(**INCORRECT**)	I work very hard, however I still find time to relax.
(CORRECT)	I work very hard. However, I still find time to relax.

However, if you overuse transitions, they can make your writing look mechanical (robotic), especially if you *always* put them at the start of a sentence. You should, therefore, vary their position (as we have done in this sentence), and don't use the same transition too often.

You can also vary your use of 'for example' and 'for instance' by moving them further down the sentence. Compare the following example sentences:

There are many ways to improve congestion. Some cities in the Netherlands, **for instance,** have pedestrian-only city centers.

There are many ways to improve congestion. Some cities in the Netherlands have pedestrian-only city centers, **for instance**.

Similarly, you can place **contrast** or **result** transitions further down the sentence:

Tokyo now has a Sky Train. Traffic problems, **as a result/therefore/as a consequence,** have decreased significantly.

Tokyo now has a Sky Train. Traffic problems have decreased significantly**, as a result/therefore/as a consequence**.

The way that you list points (first, second, third, etc.) can also be varied in order to improve your writing. For instance, they can be changed so they are no longer a transition but part of the subject. Compare the following:

Firstly, an advantage of a new public transport system is that it will reduce traffic problems.

The first advantage of a new public transport system is that it will reduce traffic problems.

Summary of common transitions			
Time	Cause/effect	Contrast	Addition
First, Second...	Therefore	However	In addition
Next	Thus	On the other hand	Moreover
Soon	Hence	In contrast	Furthermore
Then	As a result	Otherwise	Also
Finally	Consequently	Conversely	

1.15 Sentence fragments and run-on sentences

Sentence fragments

A fragment is a piece of something. For example, if you drop a glass on the floor, it will break into many fragments (separate pieces of the whole glass). A sentence fragment follows the same principle. A sentence fragment is a piece of a sentence, but not a complete sentence. A fragment might be missing a subject or a main verb, or it might express an incomplete idea. Study the following example:

> First, the effect on people's health. (**INCORRECT**)

Hopefully, you can see that there is no main verb. All we have in this example is a transition followed by a noun phrase. Therefore, this is not a complete sentence; it is a sentence fragment. This example can be corrected by simply adding a main verb and completing the idea. There are a number of ways of doing this. Study the following:

> First, the effect on people's health **is a serious concern**. (CORRECT)
>
> **The first problem is** the effect on people's health. (CORRECT)

Let's look at another example:

> In addition, showing their writing ability through well-developed essays. (**INCORRECT**)

Again, although this is a longer piece of writing, hopefully you can see that there is still no main verb. All we have in this example is a transition followed by a gerund noun phrase (showing their writing ability) and a preposition phrase (through well-developed essays). Therefore, this is not a complete sentence; it is another sentence fragment. This example can be corrected by simply adding a main verb and completing the idea. There are a number of ways of doing this.

Study the following:

> In addition, showing their writing ability through well-developed essays **takes a lot of practice.** (CORRECT)
>
> In addition, **students must practice** showing their writing ability through well-developed essays. (CORRECT)

Let's look at one final example:

> On the other hand, show a lack of ideas and development. (**INCORRECT**)

Here again, hopefully you can see that although this example has a main verb, 'show', there is no subject. Therefore, it is another sentence fragment, another incomplete sentence.

To make this into a complete sentence, we must make sure that there is a subject and a verb. There are a number of ways of doing this.

Study the following:

> On the other hand, **many students** show a lack of ideas and development. (CORRECT)
>
> On the other hand, **showing** a lack of ideas and development **is a common problem**. (CORRECT)

Run-on sentences

A run-on sentence occurs when a writer puts two or more independent clauses together in the same sentence without properly connecting them. Study the following:

> I love writing essays I don't have much time because of all my other homework.

In this example, hopefully you can see that there are actually two complete sentences that have been incorrectly combined into a single sentence. This is called a run-on sentence because the writer simply runs into the next sentence without stopping or adding a conjunction to join the two clauses.

> **Sentence 1:** I love writing essays.
>
> **Sentence 2:** I don't have much time because of all my other homework.

In addition, students sometimes attempt to connect independent clauses into a single sentence using just a comma. This is also a mistake. This type of error is called a comma splice. Study the following:

> I love writing essays, I don't have much time because of all my other homework.

Here, you can see that the writer has attempted to join the two sentences together with just a comma. Do not do this!

Some students attempt to resolve this problem by adding a transition, but as mentioned earlier, a transition cannot be used as a conjunction. Study the following example:

> I love writing essays, **however** I don't have much time because of all my other homework.

A transition has the same meaning as a conjunction (for example, the transition 'as a result' has the same meaning as the conjunction 'so', and the transition 'in addition' has the same meaning as the conjunction 'and').

However, transitions and conjunctions have very different grammatical functions. If you wish to connect independent clauses together into a single sentence, you *must* use a conjunction, not a transition. Study the following:

(INCORRECT)	I love writing essays I don't have much time because of all my other homework.
(INCORRECT)	I love writing essays**,** I don't have much time because of all my other homework.
(INCORRECT)	I love writing essays**, however** I don't have much time because of all my other homework.
(CORRECT)	I love writing essays**, but** I don't have much time because of all my other homework.
(CORRECT)	**Although** I love writing essays**,** I don't have much time because of all my other homework.
(CORRECT)	I love writing essays**. However,** I don't have much time because of all my other homework.

One final point is the use of semicolons (;). Generally, we use a semicolon to connect two sentences when a conjunction doesn't quite fit. For example, take the two sentences 'everyone needs love' and 'people need to feel like they are valued by someone'. These two sentences are clearly related, but in this instance a conjunction doesn't quite work. If we try adding a conjunction, 'Everyone needs love, and/but/so/because/when people need to feel like they are valued by someone', none of them really makes sense. In this instance, a semicolon can be used.

However, rewriting the sentence would be the better option.

> **SEMICOLON:** Everyone needs love; people need to feel like they are valued by someone.
>
> **REWRITE:** Everyone needs to feel loved and valued.

Now that we have covered the different sentence structures, transitions, and common sentence structure errors, compare the following sentences and discuss which ones are correct and which are incorrect. Be prepared to explain your answers.

1. I have a new computer studying is much easier.

2. I have a new computer, studying is much easier.

3. I have a new computer so studying is much easier.

4. I have a new computer. So, studying is much easier.

5. I have a new computer and an easier life.

6. Because I have a new computer and an easier life.

7. Because I have a new computer, so studying is much easier.

8. Because I have a new computer studying is much easier.

9. Studying is much easier because I have a new computer.

10. I have a new computer, as a result, studying is much easier.

11. I have a new computer. As a result, studying is much easier.

12. I have a new computer, and studying is much easier, as a result.

Here is a table of subordinating conjunctions and transitions. You can see that while many of these words have similar meanings, they are used differently within sentences.

Function	Subordinating conjunctions To link an independent clause with a dependent clause.	Transitions (conjunctive adverbs) To show the relationship between separate sentences in a paragraph.
Showing time and sequence	Before, As, As long as, At the same time (as), Every time, Since, The first/next/last time, When, Whenever, While, By the time, Until, After, As soon as, Ever since, Now (that)	Afterward(s), At first, Initially, Meanwhile, Simultaneously, Eventually, Finally, Nowadays, Presently, Next, Subsequently, Then, First, Firstly, Second, Secondly, Lastly, Now, At present, Today, So far, In the past, In the future, To begin with, Previously
Showing contrast or to concede a point	Although, Despite, Even though, In spite of, Instead of, Though, Whereas, While	In comparison, Conversely, However, In contrast, Instead, Nevertheless, Nonetheless, On the contrary, On the other hand, Otherwise
Showing similarity	Like, Just as	In other words, Likewise, Similarly, Equally, In the same way
To add information	X	Also, In addition, Moreover, Furthermore, Additionally, Another…
Adding example, support, emphasis	X	For example, For instance, Such as, In particular, In general, In other words, As an illustration, To put it another way, That is to say, To demonstrate, To clarify, Indeed, In fact, Namely
Showing cause	As a result of…, Because…, Due to (the fact that)…, In order to…, Since…	X
Showing effect	(If) … then, So … that	Accordingly, As a result, Consequently, Hence, Therefore, Thus, For this reason
Showing condition	Even if, If … then, In case, Provided that, Providing, Unless, Whether or not	X
To conclude	X	In conclusion, To conclude, To sum up, In summary, To summarize, In brief, Clearly, In short, In closing, To reiterate, As has been stated, Given all the above

Circle the best option from the choices in parentheses. Be prepared to explain your answers. For added practice, substitute other possible transitions in the sentences below.

1. I'm only in town for a day, (*so/ however/ therefore*) let's have lunch together.

2. My sister loves to eat, (*in contrast/ moreover/ but*) I don't care much about food.

3. That restaurant has awful food, (*for example/ for example/ despite*) the seafood.

4. She was exhausted. (*Therefore/ Nevertheless/ In fact*), she worked for another hour.

5. He studied diligently all term, (*then/ therefore/ so*) he expected to do well on the test.

6. John eats five meals a day. (*But/ Despite this/ Hence*), he never gains weight.

7. (*While/ Meanwhile/ During*) I was watching the game, the soup boiled over.

8. The music is too loud. (*Besides/ In fact/ However*), it's making the windows shake!

9. Social media can mislead people (*because/ due to/ and*) a lot of the information is untrue.

10. I like to read. Unfortunately, (*so/ but/ however*), I hardly have time to read for fun.

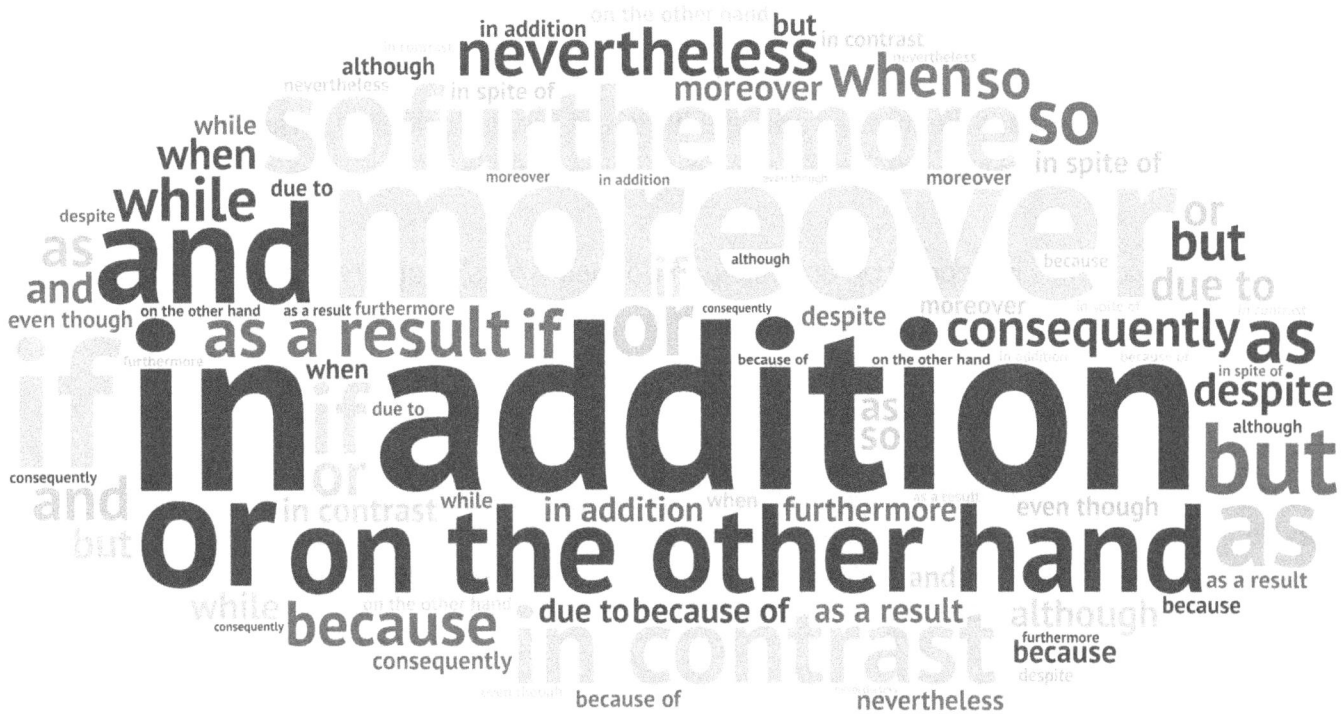

1.16 Common errors

In Chapter 1, we have covered many important aspects of writing, including countable and uncountable nouns, basic verb tenses, the seven possible sentence complements, articles, adjectives, adverbs, and the core sentence structures that you need to know. Now, correct the errors in the following sentences. Look for mistakes that have been covered so far in the book as well as some others that you should be able to find!

1. Because I studied very hard last term, so I passed the course.

2. Because their teacher cancelled class. The students are all happy yesterday.

3. My friends and I hate grammar, because of it is difficult and taking too long.

4. After class we will go out but we will do our homeworks first due to we love studying!

5. Alcohol music and dancing, they are fun but they can affect to your grades.

6. Even though, there are many student at high school go aboard to obtain their degrees, but this can be expensive and sometime stressful.

7. A clause contains a subject a verb a complement, but writing clauses are not easy as it sounds because there is so many grammar rules, and I can't remember all of it.

8. Yesterday, because I had a car's accident I was late for class miss the final exam and fail the course, however, I will retake the course for getting into college next term.

9. A healthy diet regular exercise and a relaxed hobby helps you to stay fit and happy. If you have a stress lifestyle. I work very hard, but I try to look after myself keep in shape and stay positive about life even things are difficult.

10. Every economic is depend on employee to do their works. If an economic is strong people in social are happier. Because they have more opportunity and a better quality of life. Although, it is important to be responsibility and appreciate what we have.

Now that you have looked at all ten questions, look again with the new knowledge that question 1 has one error, question 2 has two errors, question 3 has three errors, etc. (Yes, this means question 10 has ten errors!). Note also, however, that these errors include incorrect and/or missing commas.

1.17 Grammar check 1

Read the following paragraph and circle or highlight the correct answers. All the choices relate to grammar points that we have covered in Chapter 1, so refer back to the appropriate sections if you need to. Notice also that this is a carefully organized descriptive paragraph that uses some or all of the five senses (sight, smell, touch, taste, and sound) to paint a picture of the scene and enable the reader to imagine being there.

Heaven on Earth

(*Beach is, Beaches are*) a popular destination for holidaymakers, (*however, but*) Palolem Beach, in (*a, Ø, the*) India, is (*a, Ø, the*) most beautiful place I have ever been. When you arrive, you notice the fresh smell of (*sea, sea's*) air and the (*soft white, white soft*) sand between your (*toe, toes*). There (*is, are*) no (*garbages, garbage*) because the (*local, locals*) people know how important (*a, the*) beach is and keep (*there, it*) very clean. Also, there (*isn't, aren't*) too many people because (*there, it*) is not one of the major (*tourists, tourists', tourist*) destinations. (*So, As a result, However*) it is very (*peace, peaceful*). Everyone (*seem, seems*) (*relaxed, relaxing, relax*), and the (*most loud, loudest*) noise is the gentle crashing of the (*wave, waves*). If you walk down to (*a, the, Ø*) water, you can see lots of (*little beautiful, beautiful little*) shells that have been washed up onto the (*sand, sands*). (*In addition, However, Because*) the water is (*amazing, amazingly, amazed*) warm and clear. (*In fact, In contrast, Especially*) it is so clear that you can walk (*at, into, in*) the ocean for five minutes and still see the sandy bottom (*because, because of*) the water is so clear, and it is only (*two-feet deep, deep two feet*). In the distance, you can see local fishermen in (*his, their*) (*little cute wooden, cute wooden little, cute little wooden*) boats heading out to sea before (*a, the*) sun goes down. As you walk along (*a, the*) beach, you will also notice that there (*is, are*) no big hotels. (*However, Indeed, In addition*), there are no permanent (*building, buildings*) at all. All along the beach, (*small bamboo, bamboo small*) restaurants and (*beaches, beach, beach's*) huts sit between the palm (*tree, trees*), and everyone (*is, are*) either talking (*happy, happily*) or just sitting (*comfortably, comfortable*) and reading (*Ø, the, a*) book. (*Even, Although, Because*) the waiters look (*as relaxing as, as relaxed as*) the customers, but they (*are still, still are*) looking after their (*guests, guest*). I heard on (*the, Ø, a*) news (*recently, recent*) that Palolem Beach is one of (*Ø, a, the*) top ten (*beach, beaches*) in the world, so if you want to see this (*amazed, amazing*) beach, you had better hurry and buy (*a, the*) ticket today before it becomes too (*crowd, crowded*)!

1.18 Writing practice

Here are some ideas for you to practice some of the points we have covered in this chapter. We haven't really discussed paragraph development yet, but for this exercise, just state a place and choose one adjective to describe it in the first sentence. For example, "My local coffee shop is the most romantic place I have been" or "My garden is the most peaceful place I know." Then describe what you can see, hear, smell, and feel when you are in that place. To do this effectively, you should use lots of adjectives and adverbs! The *Heaven on Earth* paragraph about Palolem Beach on the previous page is a good example of a descriptive paragraph that you can use as a model.

1. Think of a specific place that would be a nice place for a date and describe it. Don't pick somewhere too big as you only have one paragraph to describe it. Just pick one café or one restaurant, for example, but your description should be detailed enough that the reader should be able to imagine being there and understand why it is a good place for a date!

2. Imagine you have a friend visiting you in your hometown for just one day. Choose the one place you think anyone visiting your city should see and describe it. Again, don't pick somewhere too big as you only have one paragraph to describe it. Just pick one landmark or important street or building, for example, but your description should be detailed enough that the reader should be able to imagine being there and understand why it is a good place to visit.

3. Choose an object (a pen, a mobile phone, a toothbrush, etc.) and write a descriptive paragraph. However, in your paragraph, do not say what it is, and see if your classmates can guess what you are describing. If you have described it well enough, your classmates should actually be able to draw exactly what you describe.

Make sure you format your writing correctly. These are general guidelines unless your instructor asks for something different.

Times New Roman size 12 font

Name and date at the top of the page

Correctly capitalized noun phrase title

Every paragraph indented using the Tab button, not the space bar

Double-spaced body text, i.e. line spacing 2.0

One-inch (2.54 cm) margin on all sides of every page

 Take the Chapter 1 Grammar Review in the supporting online material.

2. Past and present

In Chapter 1, we covered countable and uncountable nouns, basic present tenses, and sentence structures. A common problem for learners is that in English, we often switch between past tense, present tense, and future tense depending on the time frame that we are discussing. This is often true in academic writing as you need to refer to past events and research in order to draw conclusions about the present and possibly make predictions about the future. Switching between tenses can be very difficult and causes lots of problems.

The following explanations and exercises should help you to better understand the basic verb forms and how to use them more accurately.

2.1 Basic past and present tenses

Tense	Function	Example
Present Simple	Generally, present simple describes permanent situations or things that happen regularly or all the time. A present simple statement is true now, was true in the past, and will probably be true in the future.	(a) Tom **lives** in New York. (b) It **rains** a lot in England.
Past Simple	We use the past simple to talk about things that started and ended in the past: (a) short actions (b) longer situations (c) repeated events	(a) Jane **broke** her leg. (b) I **was** a naughty child. (c) I **talked** a lot in class.
Present Progressive	We use present progressive to talk about (a) a short-term activity that started in the past, is still happening *now*, and will probably continue in the future, and (b) a development or change in a general situation over a longer period of time.	(a) Jane **is sleeping**. (b) People **are smoking** less than they did fifty years ago.
Past Progressive	We use past progressive (a) to say that something was happening at a particular time in the past, and (b) to describe a longer 'background' situation that was interrupted by something.	(a) I **was watching** TV at 10 o'clock last night. (b) I **was doing** my homework when the phone rang.

The following is a list of some common *irregular* verbs.

Infinitive	Past simple	Past participle	Infinitive	Past simple	Past participle
be	was/were	been	leave	left	left
become	became	become	let	let	let
begin	began	begun	lose	lost	lost
bite	bit	bitten			
blow	blew	blown	make	made	made
break	broke	broken	mean	meant	meant
bring	brought	brought	meet	met	met
build	built	built			
buy	bought	bought	pay	paid	paid
			put	put	put
catch	caught	caught			
choose	chose	chosen	read	read	read
come	came	come	rise	rose	risen
			run	ran	run
do	did	done			
draw	drew	drawn	say	said	said
			see	saw	seen
eat	ate	eaten	sell	sold	sold
			send	sent	sent
fall	fell	fallen	shake	shook	shaken
feel	felt	felt	shine	shone	shone
find	found	found	show	showed	shown
fly	flew	flown	shut	shut	shut
forget	forgot	forgotten	sing	sang	sung
forgive	forgave	forgiven	sink	sank	sunk
			sit	sat	sat
get	got	gotten	speak	spoke	spoken
give	gave	given	spend	spent	spent
go	went	gone			
grown	grew	grown	take	took	taken
			teach	taught	taught
have	had	had	think	thought	thought
hear	heard	heard			
hide	hid	hidden	understand	understood	understood
keep	kept	kept	win	won	won
know	knew	known	write	wrote	written

It is worth noting that some verbs are rarely used in the progressive form. The following list puts these verbs into groups to make them easier to remember.

Mental and emotional states				
believe	love	doubt	hate	suppose
imagine	realize	understand	know	prefer
recognize	want	like	remember	wish
Communication and reaction				
agree	deny	impress	please	satisfy
disagree	mean	promise	surprise	believe
Others				
be	deserve	belong	need	concern
include	owe	consist	involve	contain
lack	depend	matter	own	weigh

Complete the following paragraph using any appropriate tense for the verb in parentheses. Be prepared to discuss your answers.

My New Friend

Lek (*be*) _____ my interesting new classmate this term. Before he (*start*) _____ studying here in Thailand, he (*live*) _____ in Bristol, England for two years. While he was there, he (*stay*) _____ with a nice English family, but he also (*work*) _____ in his free time for Bristol University Library. In fact, he (*meet*) _____ his girlfriend, Fon, while he (*work*) _____ in the library one weekend. Because Lek (*be*) _____ a very sociable person, he (*make*) _____ lots of amazing friends in the UK, and he still (*keep*) _____ in touch with many of them. He had to (*leave*) _____ England two months ago when his visa (*expire*) _____, and Fon (*decide*) _____ to (*return*) _____ to Thailand with him. Lek and Fon (*study*) _____ very hard at the moment because they (*want*) _____ to graduate as soon as possible. They (*stay*) _____ with Fon's parents temporarily, but they (*look*) _____ for a place of their own closer to the city because they (*need*) _____ easier access to university and all the downtown facilities.

2.2 Past perfect

As you read the paragraph below, double-underline all the main verbs. Think about the order of events. Notice how some actions happened before the day of the story, whereas other actions happened before other actions on the same day.

Red Face!

Even though I <u>was</u> only twelve years old at the time, I will never <u>forget</u> my most embarrassing moment. It was a warm summer day back in 1978, and my school had just broken up for the summer holiday. My friends and I had been playing in my back garden for a couple of hours when we decided to go inside and get a drink. When we walked into the kitchen, my brother and his friends were there with their girlfriends. They had come to watch a movie. We were all talking when I suddenly felt two hands grab my shorts and pull them down to the ground. I was suddenly half naked in front of everyone! I ran out of the kitchen and hid in my room for the rest of the day. I realized that my brother had made me look a complete fool, and from that day onwards, I have never left home without a belt!

When we are talking about the past, there are often multiple events or actions that took place either before, during, or after other events or actions in the past. In other words, when you are talking about the past there are usually other events that happened before the specific time period that you are focusing on. In this instance, past perfect is often the preferred tense. The past perfect is basically the same as present perfect, but instead of focusing on a time up to *now*, it focuses on *a time up to another time in the past*. Think of it as describing *earlier past*.

Past perfect

TIMELINE	FUNCTION	EXAMPLE
Past perfect simple PAST PRESENT FUTURE	Past perfect can express the idea that something happened (or never happened) *before another action or time in the past*.	(a) I **had already finished** my homework when my friends arrived. (b) Until yesterday, my brother **had never flown** in an airplane.
	Past perfect is common after verbs of saying and thinking to show that something happened before we thought or spoke about it.	(a) I realized that I **had forgotten** to lock the door. (b) Our teacher said that we **had all done well** on the quiz.
	When a time conjunction such as *before* or *after* is used to show that two actions happened one after the other, the past perfect is not necessary (although not wrong).	(a) I (**had**) **cleaned** the whole house before my parents came home. (b) After they (**had**) **finished** their lunch, they went shopping.
Past perfect progressive PAST PRESENT FUTURE	Past perfect progressive is commonly used to indicate the duration of a longer activity that *began in the past and continued up to another time in the past*.	(a) We **had been studying** grammar for an hour when the teacher gave us a break. (b) I **had been waiting** a week when my results finally arrived.
	Past perfect progressive can also be used without a time expression to express that something was *happening recently before* another action or time in the past.	(a) She was tired because she **had been running**. (b) The room smelled bad because someone **had been smoking**.
	Both the past perfect tenses can be used to talk about recent actions and situations in the past. The important difference is that the progressive form focuses on the activity itself, but the simple form focuses on the result.	(a) I **had been reading** all morning. (focus on activity) I **had read** both books you gave me. (focus on result)

Now, use the verbs in parentheses to complete the following sentences with any appropriate tense. Think carefully about the order of events.

1. I _____ (*see, never*) an elephant before I _____ (*come*) to Thailand last year.

2. When we _____ (*arrive*) at work this morning, we _____ (*notice*) that somebody _____ (*broke*) in and _____ (*steal*) all the computers.

3. I _____ (*meet*) my girlfriend at the shopping mall last weekend to watch a movie, but she _____ (*tell*) me that she _____ (*see, already*) the movie that I wanted to see.

4. When Jane _____ (*walk*) into the classroom, she _____ (*notice*) that the room _____ (*be*) completely empty. She _____ (*forget*) that it _____ (*be*) the day of the exam and everyone _____ (*go*) to take their exam in a different building.

5. When my brother and I _____ (*arrive*) home last night, our mother _____ (*cook*) dinner in the kitchen, and father _____ (*watch*) TV in the sitting room. However, both of them _____ (*look*) very angry like they _____ (*argue*).

46

2.3 Articles continued

Do you remember all the article rules that we covered in Chapter 1? Add appropriate articles (a, an, the, some, any) or Ø (if no article is necessary) to the following paragraph.

Shopping Trip from Hell

_____ first time I went grocery shopping alone was _____ nightmare. I was eighteen at _____ time, and I had just moved to _____ different city to study for my degree. I had never been to _____ supermarket in my life, so I knew it would be _____ interesting experience. There was _____ supermarket near _____ new house that I had just moved into, so I decided to go shopping _____ next day to buy _____ things I needed. When I entered _____ supermarket, there were _____ shopping trolleys by _____ door, but I didn't notice them, so I tried to carry everything in my arms. However, after a few minutes, my arms were full, and eventually I dropped _____ bottle of tomato sauce, which smashed on _____ floor. As I was trying to pick everything up, I bumped into _____ big stack of soup cans and knocked them over as well! Luckily, _____ employee went and got me _____ trolley to put everything in, but ten minutes later, _____ trolley was already almost full. I had bought _____ lots of food, _____ things for the kitchen and bathroom, and _____ toiletries. I tried to work out how much _____ bill would be, but I gave up and decided that it couldn't be very much. Finally, I arrived at one of _____ checkouts and began to unload all my shopping. Eventually, the cashier had scanned all my items, and my bill came pouring out of _____ machine. It was _____ mile long. I looked at _____ total and then looked at her with my mouth open and my eyes wide. It was over two hundred pounds! I began to panic. I had brought _____ money with me, but I realized that I didn't have enough to pay _____ bill! I didn't know what to do. By now, there was _____ large queue behind me, and I could sense that people were starting to get angry. Suddenly, I realized what I had to do. I pointed at something behind _____ cashier, and when she turned to look, I ran straight out of _____ shop. I never went back there again, but I learned _____ lot about London while I was trying to find _____ different supermarket.

2.4 Adjective clauses

An adjective clause (also called a relative clause) is a dependent clause used to modify a noun — to identify or give extra information about a person or thing, just like an adjective. It is a clause with a subject and a verb, but it is not the main clause.

Compare the following:

Subject pronouns Who, Which, That

Main clause 1	Main clause 2
That is a girl.	**She** gave me a valentine card.
Main clause + adjective clause	
That is **the** girl **who** gave me a valentine card.	
That is **the** girl **that** gave me a valentine card.	

In the adjective clauses above, *who* and *that* are the subjects of the adjective clause, followed immediately by the verb of the adjective clause. We can use *who* or *that* for people although *who* is considered more formal. We can never use *which* for people. Both adjective clauses have the same meaning and modify and describe the noun *girl*. Notice how, in this example, the article in the adjective clauses becomes specific (*the* not *a*) because the adjective clause tells the reader *exactly which girl* we are talking about. The adjective clause *identifies a specific girl*.

Main clause 1	Main clause 2
A game is a lot of fun.	A game involves two or more people.
Main subject + adjective clause + main verb & complement	
A game which involves two or more people is a lot of fun. (CORRECT)	
A game that involves two or more people is a lot of fun. (CORRECT)	
A game is a lot of fun that involves two or more people. (**INCORRECT**)	

Because an adjective clause adds extra information about a noun, it must always come immediately after the noun it is describing, even if it then seperates the subject from the verb in the main clause. In addition, in the examples above, notice how the article in the adjective clauses is *not* specific (*a* not *the*) because the adjective clause does not identify a specific game; it is talking about *any* game that involves two or more people, and there are lots of games that involve two or more people.

In all of these adjective clauses, *which* and *that* are the subjects of the adjective clauses, followed immediately by a verb. We can use *which* or *that* for things, although *that* is now more common if there is no comma.

Combine the following sentences using the second sentence as an adjective clause. Be sure to change the article if the adjective clause identifies a specific noun.

1. I live in a house. It was built in 1876.

   _____

2. A dog is very dangerous. It lives next door.

   _____

3. A man is standing over there. He stole your purse.

   _____

4. Some students always fall asleep in class. They sit in the back row.

   _____

5. I live next door to a family. They moved here from Brazil.

   _____

The person who guesses their secret identity is the winner.

Object pronouns Who(m), Which, That

In the second type of adjective clause, *which, that* and *who(m)* are the object of the adjective clause, not the subject. There is a subject and a verb after the pronoun, not just a verb. Notice, in the example sentences below, that the subject of each adjective clause is 'I', and the verb is 'love'. The **object** in all cases is a pronoun referring to 'the girl'. All four adjective clauses have the same meaning and are equally acceptable.

Main clause 1	Main clause 2
That is a girl.	I love **her.**
Main clause + adjective clause	
That is **the** girl **whom** I love.	
That is **the** girl **who** I love.	
That is **the** girl **that** I love.	
That is **the** girl **Ø** I love.	

In very formal English, *whom* is used as the object pronoun for people (that is the girl *whom* I love), but this is becoming less common. *Who* is now more commonly used.

Main clause 1	Main clause 2
A car is very comfortable.	I bought it yesterday.
Main subject + adjective clause + main verb & complement	
The car **which** I bought yesterday is very comfortable. (CORRECT)	
The car **that** I bought yesterday is very comfortable. (CORRECT)	
The car **Ø** I bought yesterday is very comfortable. (CORRECT)	
The car (which, that, Ø) I bought **it** yesterday is very comfortable. (**INCORRECT**)	

A very common mistake with this type of adjective clause is to include a second object in the adjective clause because the writer forgets or doesn't understand that the pronoun functions as the object in this type of adjective clause. Compare the following:

(**INCORRECT**) I have spent all the money that you gave **it** to me.
(CORRECT) I have spent all the money that you gave to me.

Finally, when the pronoun is the object of an adjective clause, we usually keep a preposition in its original position.

(**INCORRECT**) I have found a book that I was looking **for it**.
(**INCORRECT**) I have found a book that I was looking.
(CORRECT) I have found the book that I was looking **for**.

Combine the following sentences using the second sentence as an adjective clause. Again, be sure to change the article if the adjective clause identifies a specific noun.

1. Some people were nice. We met them yesterday.

   _____

2. A movie was terrible. We saw it last night.

   _____

3. A woman is extremely beautiful. You are looking at her.

   _____

4. I could not find a restaurant. You told me about the restaurant last week.

   _____

5. A library has lots of books and other resources. I visit this library most often.

   _____

I can still smell the ice-cream that my wife bought for me.

Where

Where is used in an adjective clause to modify a place — in a room, at a shop, under the bed, etc. Because *where* refers to and describes a preposition phrase, it is always followed by a subject and a verb. *Where* cannot be the subject of an adjective clause. Compare the following:

Main clause 1	Main clause 2
I live in a house.	Six other people live in my house.
Main clause + adjective clause	
I live in a house **where** six other people live.	
I live in a house **in which** six other people live.	
I live in a house **that** six other people live **in**.	
I live in a house **Ø** six other people live **in**.	

Common errors in student writing occur when they use *where* as the subject of the adjective clause, or they keep the preposition as part of the adjective clause, or they include a second reference to the place that *where* is referring to. Compare the following:

(INCORRECT)	We live in a city **where has** many people from around the world.
(INCORRECT)	We live in a city **where** many people from around the world live **in**.
(INCORRECT)	We live in a city **where** many people from around the world live **there**.
(CORRECT)	We live in a city **where** many people from around the world live.

Combine the following sentences using the second sentence as an adjective clause with *where*. Be sure to change the article if the adjective clause identifies a specific noun.

1. A hotel was very dirty. We stayed in that hotel last year.

   _____

2. This is a restaurant. We celebrated my birthday in that restaurant last year.

   _____

3. I go to a college. My parents also studied at that college.

   _____

4. A city has cleaner air. Most people in this city travel by public transport.

   _____

5. A supermarket has closed down. I do most of my shopping at that supermarket.

   _____

2.5 Punctuating adjective clauses

There are two general guidelines to follow when we punctuate adjective clauses:

1. **Do not use commas** if the adjective clause is necessary to identify the noun it modifies.

2. **Use commas** if the adjective clause simply gives extra information about the noun or statement that it modifies.

Compare the following, looking closely at how commas have been used:

1. The boy who sits next to me in class often skips class. (There are lots of boys in class, so the adjective clause is necessary in order to understand which boy.)

2. My best friend, who sits next to me in class, is asleep. (He has one best friend, so the subject is specific and the adjective clause is not required to understand which friend he is referring to. Notice also that because the adjective clause does not come at the end of the sentence, there are two commas, not just one.)

3. I always copy my homework from Jane, who sits at the front of class. (There's only one Jane, and proper nouns (names) are assumed to be specific.)

4. My math teacher is a man who comes from England. (The student only has one math teacher, but in this example, the adjective clause is describing the noun 'man' not 'my math teacher', and lots of men come from England.)

5. I sit on the back row, which makes class more fun. (The back row doesn't make it fun; the fact that *he sits on* the back row makes it fun. The adjective clause is giving information about a specific fact or situation, not a specific noun.)

If no commas are used, any possible pronoun may be used, and object pronouns may be omitted. However, if commas are necessary, the pronoun 'that' **cannot** be used and object pronouns **cannot** be omitted.

Compare the following:

(**INCORRECT**) The Lord of the Rings, **that** you lent me, was excellent. (You cannot use the pronoun *that* in an extra information adjective clause with commas.)

(**INCORRECT**) The Lord of the Rings, Ø you lent me, was excellent. (In an extra information adjective clause with commas, the object pronoun cannot be cut.)

(CORRECT) The book **that** you lent me was excellent. (The adjective clause is necessary to identify the book.)

(CORRECT) The book Ø you lent me was excellent. (Having no commas means the object pronoun can be cut.)

(CORRECT) The Lord of the Rings, **which** you lent me, was excellent. (Here the book has been named, in which case the adjective clause gives extra information and needs commas.)

Finally, sometimes an adjective clause may be separated by commas or contain no commas, with a difference in meaning. Compare the following:

1. I threw away the oranges **that** were rotten and put the others in the fridge. (Only some of the oranges were rotten.)

2. I threw away the oranges**, which** were rotten**,** so I will have to go to the market and buy some more. (All the oranges were rotten.)

Having no commas means that the adjective clause is specifying exactly *which* oranges we threw away; it tells us that only *some* of the oranges were rotten. In the second example, having commas gives extra information about *all* the oranges; the adjective clause therefore tells us that *all* of the oranges were rotten.

Now try to complete the following sentences with 'which' or 'that', and decide whether the adjective clauses require commas or not.

1. I love elephants _____ are the world's largest land animal.

2. I feel sorry for elephants _____ live in cities.

3. My sister loves Dumbo _____ is a famous Disney elephant.

4. Dumbo is an elephant _____ can fly.

5. Thailand has many elephants _____ is one reason why many tourists visit.

2.6 Adjective clause error correction

Find and correct any errors in the adjective clauses in the following sentences. Be careful — some sentences may contain more than one mistake.

1. One of the students which sits next to me never does his homework.

2. London, which it is my hometown, is a very busy place.

3. Have you read the books, which I gave them to you?

4. The hotel was very expensive, that we stayed at for our anniversary.

5. Mr. Jones is very strict which none of the students likes it.

6. Many students in this class have a car that means parking is often a problem.

7. In my old school, there were many students went to university to do their degrees.

8. Bangkok where has extremely bad traffic can be a very hot and busy place.

9. The man who wrote my English textbook for this class, he looks like my father.

10. There are people from all around the world live in New York that makes it an extremely interesting city to live in.

2.7 Noun clauses

Whereas an adjective clause *describes* a noun, a noun clause *is* a noun. It is a clause with a subject and a verb, but it is not a main clause; it is a clause that acts as a noun within a sentence — hence the name. Noun clauses begin with words such as *how, that, what, whatever, when, where, whether, which, whichever, who, whoever, whom, whomever,* and *why,* so they often look like adjective clauses, but they are not. Because they act as nouns, noun clauses can be sentence subjects, direct objects, indirect objects, predicate nominatives, or objects of a preposition.

Study the following examples:

>Everyone knows **that grammar is difficult**.
>
>>(*that grammar is difficult* is a noun clause. It contains the subject *grammar* and the verb *is*. This noun clause acts as the direct object of the sentence.)
>
>Do you know **what the weather will be like**?
>
>>(*What the weather will be like* is a noun clause. It contains the subject *weather* and the verb phrase *will be*. This noun clause also acts as the direct object in the sentence.)
>
>**Whoever thought of that idea** is a genius.
>
>>(*Whoever thought of that idea* is a noun clause. It contains the subject *whoever* and the verb *thought*. This noun clause acts as the subject in the sentence.)
>
>On weekends, we can do **whatever we want**.
>
>>(*Whatever we want* is a noun clause. It contains the subject *we* and the verb *want*. This clause acts as the direct object in the sentence.)
>
>It is important to think about **why we make certain decisions**.
>
>>(*Why we make certain decisions* is a noun clause. It contains the subject *we* and the verb *make*. This clause acts as the object of the preposition *about* in the sentence.)
>
>My wife and I can't decide **whether we will go on holiday this year**.
>
>>(*whether we will go on holiday this year* is a noun clause. It contains the subject *we* and the verb *go*. This noun clause acts as the direct object in the sentence. Note that *whether* always indicates a choice of some kind.)

One common error that students make with noun clauses is to include two introductory words. Compare the following:

>(**INCORRECT**) I couldn't decide **that which** university I should attend.
>
>(CORRECT) I couldn't decide which university I should attend.

Another common mistake is to write the noun clause as a question. Compare the following:

>(**INCORRECT**) He didn't understand why **should he** study in the evenings.
>
>(CORRECT) He didn't understand why **he should** study in the evenings.

Chapter 2: Past and present

Now look at the following sentences and decide which of the options best completes each sentence.

1. The government recently announced _____.

    A. where will they build the new hospital

    B. where they will build the new hospital

2. The BBC reported _____.

    A. where do most immigrants choose to live

    B. where most immigrants choose to live

3. The president declared _____.

    A. how much income he makes

    B. how much income does he make

4. _____ is not apparent yet.

    A. How close we are to achieving success

    B. How close are we to achieving success

5. _____ was extremely concerning.

    A. What did the newspaper report about the Prime Minister

    B. What the newspaper reported about the Prime Minister

Study the following paragraph. Highlight and label all adjective clauses and noun clauses. Be prepared to discuss the differences.

Whoever visits my local restaurant should be careful how they order. The Blue Lobster, which opened about a year ago, says that it has the best seafood in town, but the food that I received was not what I expected. The waiter asked my wife and I what we wanted, but he didn't make a note of our order. In fact, he boasted that he has an amazing memory and never writes down people's orders. About 20 minutes later, he brought two dishes to our table, but the food he brought was definitely not what we had ordered. When we told him that he had brought the wrong food, he smiled and said that he had brought us something even better! We have never been back to the Blue Lobster, but we often eat at the restaurant next door, where they get our order right.

2.8 Reported speech

Direct speech (quoting)

In your writing, especially in academic essays in which you use other people's information and ideas, you must understand how and when to quote or paraphrase other people. Using quotation marks (" "), we can provide a person's or organization's exact words in support of a point we are trying to make. This method of reporting speech is called *direct speech,* and it is best used when the wording is important. For example, when you use a respected expert's opinion or an official definition to support your essay, then the wording will be very carefully chosen to communicate a precise message. In this case, it would be inappropriate and unwise for us to try and reword the statement as we might accidentally alter the exact meaning.

In the following examples, notice that a quote always starts with a capital letter if it is a full sentence that is being quoted, or a small letter if it is only part of a sentence that is being used. A quote is always separated from the rest of the sentence with a comma. For example:

> Mayo Clinic defines gambling addiction as**,** "the uncontrollable urge to keep gambling despite the toll it takes on your life."

In the example above, the wording is particularly important as an official definition of a serious issue from a respected source, so quoting the exact words is better.

When we put a reporting phrase after a quote (rather than before it), the subject usually comes after the reporting verb unless the subject is a pronoun.

> "Gambling puts families at risk," **stated the minister.**

> "Gambling puts families at risk," **he stated**.

Reporting expressions often interrupt the quote.

> "Gambling puts families at risk," **he stated**, "and my goal is to stamp it out."

Indirect speech (paraphrasing)

Making another person's words part of our own sentence is called *indirect speech*. We can introduce another person's information with the conjunction *that* (although in many cases *that* is omitted). It is best to paraphrase a sentence when it is the information that is important, not the wording. However, we must be careful not to alter the meaning of the original information as we rewrite it in our own words. For example:

> Original statement: "Americans lost $119 billion from gambling last year."

Here, the wording is not particularly important; it is the information that is important, so it is best to paraphrase:

> The minister **said** (that) gambling had cost Americans nearly $120 billion last year.

As a fun example of how easily information can change as it passes from person to person, have a quick round of the telephone game. One person starts by whispering a sentence to the person next to them. That person then tries to remember the sentence and whisper it to another person, and so on to the end of the chain. The last person in the chain then says the sentence out loud to the whole group, and you will see how messages easily change as they pass from person to person.

Adverbs of time and place often have to be altered:

My brother called me and said, "I am getting married **tomorrow**."

My brother called me and said (that) he was getting married **the next day**.

now	=	then
yesterday	=	the previous day/the day before
today	=	that day
tomorrow	=	the following day/the next day
ago	=	before

Usually, we change the verb tense to agree with the introductory clause, as in (a) below.

However, if the speech you are reporting is probably still true now, you do not need to change the verb to past tense, as in (b).

(a) My brother told me (that) he ***didn't feel*** well.   (Verb is changed to past tense because he might feel fine today)

(b) My brother told me (that) his wife *is* very beautiful.   (Present tense is maintained because he probably still thinks she's beautiful)

In reported questions and answers, the subject usually comes before the verb, and the auxiliary *do* is not used.

Compare the following:

"How do you feel about the situation?" he asked.

(INCORRECT)   He asked **how did I felt** about the situation.

(INCORRECT)   He asked **how did I feel** about the situation.

(CORRECT)   He asked **how I felt** about the situation.

Is becomes *was*, *will* becomes *would*, *can* becomes *could*, etc., but modal verbs *would*, *should*, *could*, *might*, and *must* remain unchanged in reported speech.

He said, "You **should** come to the wedding."

He told me (that) I **should** go to the wedding.

When reporting a question that does not have a question word such as *who*, *what*, *where*, and *how*, we use *if* or *whether* to connect the reported question.

"**Will you** be at the wedding?" he asked.

He asked **if/whether I would** be at the wedding.

Now you try! Yesterday, you spoke to an old friend, but today you are talking to a different friend. Use both direct and indirect speech to report what your friend from yesterday said. Remember, this meeting only happened yesterday, so some of the information is probably still true today.

1. How are you? (he asked)

   Quote: He asked, "How are you?" or "How are you?" he asked.

   Paraphrase: He asked how I **was**. (NOT He asked how I **am**)

2. Where do you work? (he asked)

   Quote: _____

   Paraphrase: _____

3. I work at a bank, but I have the day off today. (you said)

   Quote: _____

   Paraphrase: _____

4. Would you like go out for dinner? (he asked)

   Quote: _____

   Paraphrase: _____

2.9 Sentence structure: review

Let's now review and see how much you remember about sentence structure. In the parentheses at the end of each sentence, please label the type of sentence structure (simple, compound, complex, compound/complex).

To help you do this, underline subjects, double-underline main verbs, and put a + sign above all conjunctions. Also, place brackets around and identify all the 'chunks' of grammar that are used in each sentence.

My Greatest Achievement

The proudest moment (of my life) happened when my school's football team
     noun phrase   prep. phrase   +   noun phrase

played (in the regional league) (Complex). We had never played in the league
    prep. phrase

before because our school was quite small (_____). However, our teacher thought that we were good enough, so he applied for us to play in the season (_____). During the competition, we had to play 32 other teams over a two-month period to progress to the finals (_____). We were lucky in the first few rounds because we played teams from smaller schools (_____). In later rounds, however, we played some better teams from bigger schools with older boys (_____). These matches were difficult because they were stronger and faster than us, but we fought hard and won (_____). Eventually, we progressed to the final match, and we were very nervous (_____). The game lasted 90 minutes, and the team that we played was quite famous in our local area (_____). It was the hardest match that we had ever played, and after 90 minutes, the score was 2:2 (_____). The game went to penalties to decide the winner (_____). I had never taken a penalty shot in a real match, and I was the last one to shoot, so I was extremely nervous, but I stayed calm and aimed for the top corner of the goal (_____). I scored (_____)! We won the match, and my proudest memory was created (_____).

2.10 Paragraph development

Now that we have covered basic grammar and sentence structures, it is time to start talking about how to write more than just one sentence.

In English, if we want to explain a simple idea, then a single sentence may be enough. However, if we want to explain something more complex, we may require a collection of sentences that all work together to explain the main idea. We call this a paragraph.

On the other hand, if the point you want to explain is even more complex, then a single paragraph may not be enough, and you may require a collection of paragraphs all working together. We call this an essay.

The thing to remember is that each paragraph must have a single idea, and all the information within the paragraph must work together to explain this idea. Paragraphs can sometimes become confusing if the writer doesn't plan, introduce, and explain their ideas clearly.

One way to ensure that the reader understands the main idea of a paragraph is to start it with a topic sentence — the main idea of a paragraph stated clearly at the start of the paragraph so that the reader does not have to figure it out for themselves as they read.

Topic sentences

A topic sentence contains two parts: a topic and a controlling idea. The topic is the thing that you will write about (cats, computers, your bedroom, etc.), and the controlling idea is what you will say about that thing (fun for kids, help students, beautiful, etc.). Compare the following topic sentences introducing different paragraphs about the same topic — computers:

Topic	Controlling idea	Paragraph type
Computers	help students with their studies.	**Cause/effect**
Computers	changed my life when I was 14.	**Narrative**
Computers	are a beautiful addition to any office.	**Descriptive**
Computers	are easy to update if you follow these steps.	**Process**
Computers	are better than books for three reasons.	**Compare/contrast**

A good topic sentence leaves the reader with a question in their mind, and the job of the paragraph is to answer that question. For example, when a reader reads the topic sentence *computers help students*, the question in their mind will be: "How do computers help students?" As a result, it is very important that you don't start talking about something different. For example, if you are discussing how computers help students, you should *not* start talking about playing games or doing business on computers.

It is important that you narrow your topic to something specific enough for a single paragraph. For example, *technology* is too general to write about in a single paragraph. You need to choose one kind of technology, such as *mobile phones*, *computers*, or *the internet*, and it is important to make your controlling idea specific enough to be explained in a single paragraph. For example, *has many benefits*, although not exactly wrong, is probably too general to be explained in just 4–12 sentences. You need to choose one benefit such as *help a child's development*, *improve international business*, or *assist students with their English*.

Read the following paragraphs and, for each one, add a suitable topic sentence to introduce the main idea. Remember, your topic sentence must be a sentence, not a verb phrase or noun phrase.

_____

One reason for the low-quality air in this city is the number of cars and other vehicles on the roads every day. This situation is made even worse by the fact that many of these vehicles are old and inefficient. This results in toxic gases that harm human health and cause climate change. Another factor is that Mexico City is surrounded by mountains and lies 2,240 meters above sea level. This geographic location makes it much harder for the wind to blow pollution out of the city. These are the main reasons for the terrible air quality in Mexico City.

_____

First, boil about half a liter of water. While the water is heating up, put a tea bag in a tea pot and add a small amount of milk into each tea cup. You should also prepare a small bowl of sugar in case people prefer their tea to be a bit sweet. Once the water has boiled, pour it into the teapot, put the lid on, and cover it with the tea cozy to keep the tea hot while it brews. Finally, after 5 minutes (no less and no more), the tea is ready to pour into the cups and add sugar as desired. You and your guests can now enjoy a lovely cup of tea.

_____

On the one hand, my old house was really quite big. We even had spare rooms inside the house that we used as a games room and for storage. Even my bedroom was quite large with enough space for me to have a small desk area for me to do my homework in private. The only negative about this house was the location as it took at least an hour to get to school, and my parents seemed to take a long time to commute to and from work every day. On the other hand, my new house is a little bit smaller, but it is still comfortable and clean. The biggest difference is the location as I can now get to school in five minutes! My parents also seem much happier because they spend less time in their cars every day and can spend more time with me at home.

2.11 Narrative paragraphs

A narrative paragraph is a short story, with a beginning, a middle, and an end. It might be a sad story, a happy story, an adventure story, a scary story — anything, but the reader should not know the climax of the story until the end!

You have already read two narrative paragraphs (two stories) in Chapter 2: *Red Face* (an embarrassing story when the author's brother pulled his shorts down) and *My Greatest Achievement* (a story about winning a school football tournament).

As you read the following explanations, refer back to the example stories and study how they have been written.

Topic sentence

The first thing you must write for a narrative paragraph is the topic sentence introducing what your story will be about. Be careful not to simply write a fact or reveal the end the story before the reader has had chance to read it! Your topic sentence should leave the reader curious and wanting to know what happened. Your story might be scary, proud, shocking, embarrassing, cute, etc., but your topic sentence must reflect and introduce this without giving away too much information or telling the reader how the story ends.

Background

After the topic sentence, you should write one or two background sentences to build up a picture in the reader's mind of the time, place, characters, and the general situation (who, what, when, where, why) before you begin the actual story. When you read a good book or watch a good movie, the first 20–30% always introduces the characters, the location, the time period, etc. in order to set the scene before the actual story, the series of connected events, happens.

Event

Once you have written a few background sentences, you can begin the actual event, the thing that happened, the story. Be careful that you don't simply describe a situation in the past; a story is a series of things that happen in time order with a result at the end.

A good story should always build up to a single exciting, shocking, scary, funny, or romantic event. If there is no event, just a series of everyday chores or activities such as waking up, having breakfast, walking on the beach and going to bed, then your story is not a very good one. Think of something interesting!

Conclusion

Finally, you can write the end of the story, the conclusion. The easiest way to write a conclusion is simply to restate the topic sentence — to say the same thing but in different words. However, a more imaginative way to conclude your paragraph might be to say what the main character of your paragraph learned from the experience, or how they reacted or changed in response to the experience. For example, in our first story *Red Face*, the author has always worn a belt since his brother pulled his shorts down and embarrassed him.

Study the following narrative paragraph. Notice how the topic sentence introduces the main idea of the story and the structure of the paragraph follows the narrative paragraph guidelines from the previous page.

Try labelling all the main verbs for extra practice as well.

Birthday of a Lifetime

(**Topic sentence**) The day I asked my girlfriend to marry me will always be the most terrifying day of my life. (**Background**) It was June 27th 2002, my girlfriend's birthday, and we had been going out with each other for two years. I had bought a beautiful ring the week before and arranged everything with her family. (**Event**) On the day of her birthday, I took my girlfriend, Jane, shopping. While she was enjoying looking around, I was getting more and more nervous. I kept looking at my watch and thinking about what I was going to say. At 7:30, I asked her if she was hungry and told her I had booked us a table in a nice restaurant. I was not hungry at all. In fact, I felt sick. When we walked in, all of Jane's family were there waiting, and she started crying. I was so nervous I had trouble just standing up! "There is actually one more present," I whispered in her ear. I felt faint. I asked her to sit down, and the room went quiet. She looked around confused, and began to shake when she saw me put one knee on the floor. "Jane, will you marry me?" I asked. She looked at me with tears in her eyes. I had never seen her look so scared. "It's too quick," she whispered. My whole world went dark, and I nearly fell over. I cannot remember what I said next, but I know that it must have been the right thing to say because everyone started clapping and smiling, and I was holding Jane's hand and showing everyone the ring on her finger. I had done it! (**Conclusion**) We have been happily married for the last 20 years, but whenever I have something important that I want to ask, I always think very carefully before speaking!

2.12 Grammar check 2

Read the following narrative paragraph and circle the correct answers. Be prepared to explain your answers. Notice also that this is another narrative paragraph (a story) with a topic sentence, background information, and an event.

My First Date

My first date was the most (*terrified, terrifying*) day of my life! I was fourteen years old, and I (*had liked, liked*) a girl (*who, which*) studied in my class, Jenny, for at least a year before. I was quite (*Ø, a, the*) shy young boy, (*but, and, therefore*) it (*had taken, had took, took*) all my courage to (*asked, ask*) her (*if she would, that would she*) like to see (*the, a, Ø*) movie with me. On (*the, a*) day of the date, I went to the hairdresser, (*and, Ø*) prepared my best (*cloth, cloths, clothes*), and spent all my time (*thought, thinking, to think*) about what I (*will, would*) say to her. I (*had, have*) never been so nervous! We (*agreed, had agreed, have agreed*) to meet at (*a, the*) cinema at eight o'clock, (*but, so, however*) I arrived an hour early! Finally, she arrived, at exactly eight. She (*had looked, looked*) beautiful! I was (*very, so, too*) nervous that I dropped my *popcorn*. (*But, In addition, However*), she smiled and walked (*into, at, towards*) me. "Hi," I said, "You (*looked, look*) great!" I felt my face (*turn, turned*) red. She asked (*if I had been waiting, that was I waiting*) long, but I told her that I (*arrived, had been arriving, had arrived*) just five minutes (*ago, before*). Eventually, we went (*in, to, into*) the cinema and sat down. (*A, The*) movie started, (*and, but, nevertheless*) I couldn't (*follow, followed*) the story (*because, during, because of*) I was thinking so hard about how I could put my arm around her. Eventually, I made my move. I pretended to yawn (*and, Ø*) brought my right arm down (*for resting, to rest*) around her shoulders. I stayed exactly like that for (*a, the*) next hour. When the movie eventually finished, (*so, because, Ø*) Jenny stood up (*for leaving, to leave*), and I realized that I (*spent, had spent, was spending*) the last hour with my arm around (*a, the*) back of her chair. I hadn't even (*touched, touch*) her shoulders! Outside (*a, the*) cinema, Jenny's mother (*waited, was waiting*) for us. We both jumped in the car, and after a (*twenty-minute, twenty minutes*) ride, I arrived home. I thanked Jenny's mother (*then, and*) ran into my house! We ended up (*to date, dating*) each other for a year, but I (*had, will, have*) never forgotten how (*embarrassed, embarrassing*) my first date was.

2.13 Writing practice

Here are some ideas for you to practice some of the points we have covered in this chapter. Use this opportunity to practice all the language that you have learned so far in the book. Think carefully about your nouns and sentence structures.

Try to include lots of adjectives and adverbs in your story in order to build a more detailed picture in the reader's mind and add detail to your story. Also, for practice, see if you can include examples of past perfect and reported speech.

1. Write about your most embarrassing experience.
2. Write about the naughtiest thing you have ever done.
3. Write about the scariest experience of your life.
4. Write about the first time you tried to do something you had never done before.
5. Write about the first time you went out at night with your friends.

Remember to format your paragraph correctly unless your instructor asks for something different:

Times New Roman size 12 font

Name and date at the top of the page

Correctly capitalized noun phrase title

Every paragraph indented using the Tab button, not the space bar

Double-spaced body text, i.e. line spacing 2.0

One-inch (2.54 cm) margin on all sides of every page

 Take the Chapter 2 Grammar Review in the supporting online material.

3. Introduction to essays

As mentioned in Chapter 2, we write a paragraph to explain a single relatively simple idea. However, we write essays to explore and explain a more complex idea. Because this involves writing much more, we break the whole piece of writing into more manageable, bite-size pieces called paragraphs, with each piece being an individual part of the bigger picture — a series of paragraphs dealing with different aspects of a larger issue. In this diagram, you can see how a writer uses the same organization of ideas but expands the piece of writing into a standard five-paragraph essay in order to more fully explain each point.

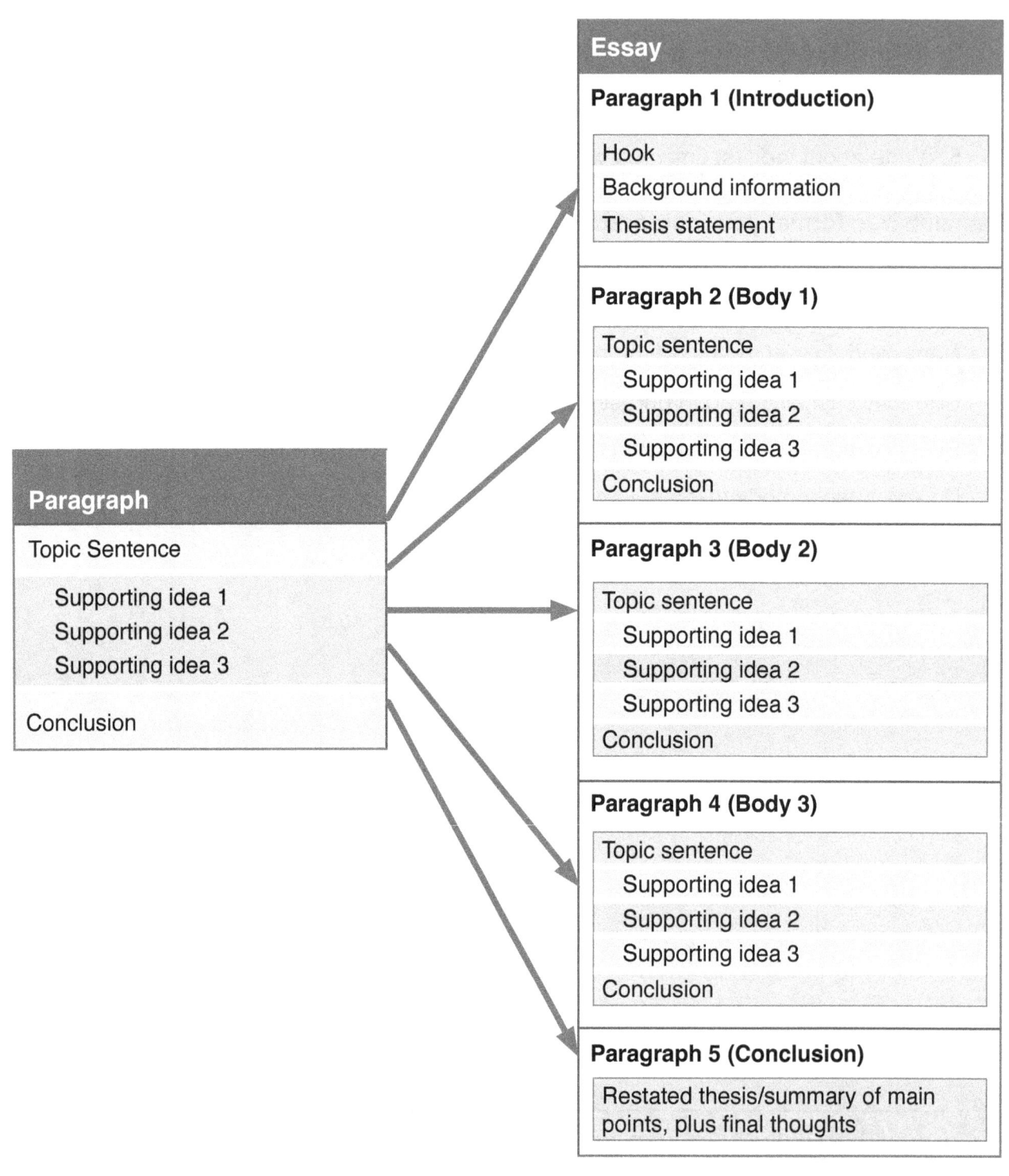

3.1 Introductions

A good introduction should capture the reader's interest, identify your topic, provide essential background context, and indicate the particular focus of your essay in the thesis statement. Some students cannot begin writing the body of the essay until they feel they have the perfect introduction, but beware of spending too much time on the introduction, and not enough time planning and writing the main body of your essay.

When you are first given an essay topic, you should brainstorm all aspects of the issue to determine the most important factors. For example, with an argumentative topic (a topic that people disagree about), once you have brainstormed both sides of the issue, you can start to eliminate and organise the different ideas from your brainstorm into major categories, which you can then use to organize your different paragraphs and supporting ideas. Once you have all this information, you are in a much better position to write your introduction and thesis statement. In other words, it is difficult to write a good introduction until you have planned your essay.

Once you have completed your brainstorm and outline, consider these strategies for writing an effective introduction:

    1. Find a surprising statistic or an interesting quote that illustrates the importance of the issue that you will discuss.

    2. Give some general background information necessary for understanding the topic of your essay by briefly explaining *who, what, when, where,* and *why* this is an issue and *how* it developed over time.

Once you have introduced the topic of your essay and given a bit of background information, you must end your introduction paragraph with a thesis statement that puts forward the main idea of your essay. One major mistake that students often make is to copy the assignment prompt (the essay instructions/question) using the exact same wording. *You must not do this*!

Your thesis statement can be either *indirect* or *direct*, depending on how much you want to help your reader understand your ideas. An *indirect thesis statement* says the main idea of your essay but doesn't give any clues about what your main points will be. A *direct thesis statement*, on the other hand, gives the main idea of you essay, but it also tells the reader the main supporting points that you will be discussing.

A direct thesis statement is therefore better because it gives the reader a good understanding of the main points that will be covered before they get into the body paragraphs. Study the following examples:

    a. Primary school students should not be given a mobile phone for two reasons.

Here, the reader knows that the essay will be against children having phones, but the reader doesn't know what each paragraph will talk about. This is an *indirect thesis statement*.

    b. Primary school students should not be given a mobile phone because they will not concentrate on their studies and they may be exposed to inappropriate content.

In the second example, the reader knows that this essay will not support children owning phones, but they also know exactly what each supporting paragraph will talk about. This is called a *direct thesis statement*. It tells the reader what each paragraph or section of your essay will discuss.

3.2 Body paragraphs

The following strategies will help you write body paragraphs that will be appropriate to the writing task, provide appropriate evidence to prove your thesis, and also show off your writing skills.

The following list gives the most useful evidence strategies you can use. Not every evidence strategy fits the purpose of every writing task, so learn and practice these options to increase your ability to support your different ideas.

Evidence strategies

　1. A fact is something that is known to exist or to have happened.

　2. An experience used as evidence may be a commonly known event or an event of which there is limited knowledge.

　3. A comparison or a contrast shows how the subject is similar to or different from something else in a meaningful way.

　4. Logic means using deductive (general to specific) or inductive (specific to general) reasoning to explain what evidence proves and how it relates to the topic you are talking about.

　5. A counter-argument states an opinion that disagrees with your thesis statement, which you can then go on to disprove or at least weaken in order to support the quality of your own argument.

Body paragraphs are organized around the topic sentence, each of which is one of the main points, reasons, or arguments in support of the thesis statement.

In other words, each paragraph has a main idea of its own, but all of the body paragraphs together support and explain the main idea of the essay — the thesis statement. Always place your topic sentence at the beginning of each body paragraph.

Research indicates that the topic sentence is placed at the beginning of the body paragraph 80% of the time in published works, so don't re-invent the wheel. Write in the way your reader expects to read by clearly introducing the main idea of each paragraph with a topic sentence.

After composing the topic sentence for a body paragraph, you must provide multiple reasons, evidence, and explanations to prove that your main idea is true. From the evidence strategies above, using two or three types of evidence per body paragraph is more effective and makes the paragraph much stronger, whereas limiting evidence to just one idea or one form of evidence will weaken your overall argument.

The more points and evidence that you have, the more likely you are to persuade your reader that you are correct!

Remember to connect your body paragraph supporting points and evidence strategies with effective transition words to maintain coherence and ensure that your ideas and explanations flow together as one whole.

Every word should move the reader toward agreeing with the main idea of your paragraph, and all your paragraphs should work together to support the main idea of your essay.

3.3 Counter-arguments

In this book, we will start with a very useful but quite tricky essay to master — the argumentative essay. Very often in English writing tests and exams, you are asked your opinion about something. The topic is often something that people have different opinions about. In this situation, it is necessary to have your own opinion about the topic, but it is also very effective to show consideration of other people's opinions. A counter-argument is opposite to your opinion. It expresses the view of a person or group of people who disagree with your position.

Why use counter-arguments?

If it is done well, a counter-argument paragraph makes your own arguments and the essay as a whole stronger. This is because it gives you the chance to respond to your reader's objections before they have finished reading your essay. It also shows that you are a reasonable person who has considered both sides of a debate. Both of these factors make your essay more intelligent, balanced, and persuasive.

How should the counter-argument be introduced?

It's important to use clear language to signal to the reader that you are about to express a view that is different from your own opinion. The purpose of this type of paragraph is to show that you have considered the opposing viewpoint, but then eventually change your opponents' mind and persuade them to support your opinion. As a result, clear language is crucial in order to guide the reader carefully from one opinion to another. If this is not done carefully, the paragraph appears incoherent, contradictory, and confusing. Generally, the counter-argument will begin with a word, phrase or sentence to indicate that what follows is *not* your view. In general, the strategy is to make it clear that this is someone else's opinion, *not* yours. Typical introductory strategies include the following:

> On the other hand, many/ some/ a few people believe/ argue/ feel/ suppose/ etc. that (state the counter-argument here).

> Despite the aforementioned benefits/ drawbacks, it is often thought/ imagined/ supposed/ believed/ etc. that (state the counter-argument here).

Notice how, in each sentence introducing a counter-argument statement, we use verbs like *imagine*, *believe*, and *feel* to make their opinion sound weak. This is important because later in the paragraph, we will attempt to argue against these people and change their mind on the issue.

How should you refute the counter-argument?

As mentioned, the counter-argument requires careful signaling to ensure that the reader understands that this is the opinion of someone else, *not* your opinion. Now, however, we will attempt to argue against these people and change their mind. This is called your refutation. It is essentially your reply to your opponent's counter-argument.

Confused? You can see why you must do this carefully so that your reader will not become confused as well. Essentially, your essay must do a 180° turn away from its thesis as you address your opponent's main argument against you, and then you must do another 180° change of direction to reply to your opponent's counter-argument and hopefully change their mind. The reader needs clear language and guidance, or they will get lost.

As a result, you need transitional language to indicate that you are going to refute this argument and that you have returned to arguing your own opinion. Study the following:

> In other words, opponents believe that…, but in reality, (refute counter-argument here).

> In other words, opponents believe that … However, evidence shows that… (refute counter-argument here).

> Opponents may claim that… However, although this position is popular and might sound reasonable, the facts support my argument that (refute counter-argument here).

If we put all this together, we end up with a paragraph that introduces and explains the main argument against our own position, but then the paragraph goes on to refute that argument by explaining why their point is weak or wrong and/or how their counter-argument can be mitigated. Study the following example counter-argument paragraph for an essay that argues against evening classes for children. Remember — in this example, the essay as a whole is arguing that evening classes are *negative*, but in the following paragraph, the writer wants to address the main argument from people who think that evening classes are *positive*.

> Despite the aforementioned drawbacks of evening classes, supporters argue that children need to learn a lot more these days and evening classes are the only way to achieve this. These people claim that increased competition and higher standards mean that their children must study in the evenings in order to be successful. However, although this argument may appear reasonable at first glance, these parents do not appreciate the value of play and relaxation for children. Stress and even depression have become growing concerns in today's world, including among children. The pressure to get high grades can be extremely intense, and this has led to a sharp increase in mental disorders and even suicide. In addition, play and relaxation also form part of a child's education as they learn to interact with others and become happy and healthy members of society.

After reading this paragraph, who wins? Hopefully, you can see that the writer has dealt with the main argument in support of evening classes (*against* the main idea of the essay) *and* shown why those people are wrong to support evening classes for their stated reason.

3.4 Conclusions

A strong conclusion will provide a sense of closure to the essay while again placing your ideas in a wider context. An effective conclusion allows the reader to close the door on the topic as it summarizes and completes the essay in the reader's mind. It will also, in some instances, encourage further thought on the subject. However, a conclusion is not merely a summary of your points or a re-statement of your thesis. If you wish to summarize, do this in fresh language. Remind the reader how the evidence you presented has contributed to your thesis and proven your main idea to be true. The conclusion, like the rest of the paper, involves critical thinking. Reflect on the significance of your essay and try to convey some meaningful closing thoughts about the issue.

How do I write an interesting and effective conclusion?

The following strategies may help you move beyond merely summarizing the key points of your essay:

1. If your essay deals with a contemporary problem, warn readers of the possible consequences of not addressing the problem.

2. Recommend a specific course of action that might solve the issue.

3. Use an appropriate quotation or expert opinion to lend authority to the conclusion you have reached.

4. Return to an anecdote, example, or quotation that you introduced at the start of your essay, but add further insight that comes from the body of your essay.

5. In a science or social science paper, mention worthwhile possibilities for future research on your topic.

3.5 Essay structure: review

Does all that make sense? How much do you remember? See how many of the following questions you can answer:

1. What is the purpose of an essay?

2. How many paragraphs can an essay have?

3. What is the purpose of the introduction?

4. How should the introduction end?

5. What is a direct thesis statement? Give an example.

6. What is an indirect thesis statement? Give an example.

7. What is a topic sentence? In published works, how frequently is the topic sentence the first sentence of a paragraph?

8. How many types of evidence should you use in each paragraph?

9. What types of evidence can you use in your body paragraphs?

10. Other than restating the thesis and summarizing your key points (in 'fresh language'), what should you include in your conclusion?

3.6 Putting theory into practice

Let's take an example topic and run through the essay-writing process together. Take a look at this essay prompt. What kind of essay would you write?

> Many children are required to participate in community activities such as looking after the elderly or cleaning their local area as a part of their education. Do you think schools should include this type of activity in their curriculum, or not? Support your answer with reasons and explanations.

Think about it. What is the topic? What is the question asking for? Where would you start? Would you start writing now, or do you need to brainstorm and plan first?

First of all, many students start by copying the prompt, word for word, at the top of their page, but you should *never* do this. Your teacher or the examiner has already seen the essay prompt, so they do not need to see it again. You should also avoid copying chunks of language from the prompt to use in the body of your essay. Many students use the exact wording from the prompt or parts of the prompt throughout their essay, sometimes multiple times, but this looks very bad as it is someone else's language, not your own! You can use the same vocabulary, but try not to use the exact same phrases, clauses or sentences as the prompt.

Where do we begin? Well, community work for school children is clearly a topic that people have different opinions about. Some people support it, whereas other people are against it. As a result, we could write an essay that discusses both sides of the debate, or an essay that supports one side but also includes the opposing opinion in order to argue against it.

Let's start by brainstorming ideas for both sides of the issue. Complete the table below with as many arguments as you can think of. Don't worry about spelling or complete sentences. Just note down as many arguments for and against the topic as you can think of. Many students stop once they have one or two main ideas for each side, but please dig deeper and try to think of all the arguments for each side of the debate.

Advantages of community service	Disadvantages of community service
1.	1.
2.	2.
3.	3.
4.	4.
5.	5.
6.	6.
7.	7.
8.	8.

Hopefully, you spent a bit of time brainstorming ideas on the previous page. Critical thinking is an essential skill, but it takes practice! Many students don't spend enough time on the brainstorm, or they just skip it completely. However, the brainstorm is essential in order to get all our ideas out there and think deeply about the issue before we organize everything into an outline and then write our essay.

Here is an example brainstorm:

Advantages of community service	Disadvantages of community service
Learn outside school	Academic subjects more important
Have fun with friends	Dangerous
Experience	Tiring
Help less fortunate people	Boring
Keep our community clean	Waste of time
Learn new skills	Have to travel far
Teamwork	Not fun
Learn to care about other people	Not learning anything
Become more responsible	Government responsibility
See the real world	Working with strangers
Enjoy working with others	Chaotic and hard to manage
Make new friends	Accidents
Better communication skills	Fights and arguments
Learn from older generations	Takes all day not just one class
Looks good on a resume	
Experience daily chores	
Time management	

From the brainstorm, it seems like there are more reasons to support community work than against it. Also, some of the arguments against it are not very strong arguments such as 'boring' and 'not fun', so we should choose to write an essay that supports children participating in community work.

Now that we have our brainstorm, is it time to start writing? No, it isn't. We have some nice ideas here, but we need to edit and organize them into a quick outline before we start writing our essay. Quickly outlining your essays means that you do not have to worry about what to write next as you are writing.

Many students who try to write their essays without planning them first have to think about content and grammar at the same time, which usually leads to lower-quality essays.

Plan first so that you can focus mainly on grammar and sentence structure as you write your essay.

Chapter 3: Introduction to essays

In the following table, you can see that similar arguments have been grouped together into rough categories. These categories (in bold) can be the main ideas of different paragraphs and the other ideas can be the supporting points inside each paragraph.

Advantages of community service	Disadvantages of community service
See the real world	**Academic subjects more important**
Learn outside school	Not learning anything
Have fun with friends	Waste of time
Enjoy working with others	Takes all day not just one class
Make new friends	
	Dangerous
Learn new skills	Accidents
Better communication skills	Working with strangers
Teamwork	Fights and arguments
Keep our community clean	Chaotic and hard to manage
Experience daily chores	Have to travel far
Become more responsible	Government responsibility
Help less fortunate people	
Learn to care about other people	~~Tiring~~
Learn from older generation	~~Boring~~
Looks good on a resume	~~Not fun~~
~~Experience~~	
~~Time management~~	

As part of the editing and organizing process, two advantages have been cut. First of all, 'experience' is too general. Waking up, brushing your teeth, traveling to school or work, eating, and sleeping are all experiences, so this is too general to be a specific argument for or against the topic. 'Time management' has also been cut as this is done by the teachers, not by the students. If the students have to make their own way there and organize the activities themselves, then time management would be a valid skill that they must develop, but generally this is done by the adults who organize and supervise the activities.

For the disadvantages, 'tiring', 'boring', and 'not fun' have been cut because adults would not consider these to be valid reasons not to do something. Many things can be tiring and boring but extremely important at the same time. In addition, some of the disadvantages are a bit repetitive, such as 'waste of time' and 'takes all day', and 'dangerous' and 'accidents'. Again, the similar disadvantages have been grouped into categories, which could then be developed into paragraphs if we chose to support and develop that side of the argument.

This leaves us with three main arguments to support student community work and two or three main arguments against. If time allowed and/or the task required it, we could use all of these ideas to write an eight-paragraph compare/contrast essay (including an introduction and conclusion paragraph). However, there is usually some kind of length or time limit imposed on writing assignments due to time constraints and other factors, so we need to decide which side of the debate to support, what type of essay to write, and which ideas to include or cut in order to satisfy the word-count requirement within the time limit.

First of all, as previously stated, the ideas supporting community work are stronger than the arguments against. This makes an argumentative essay a good choice as it allows us to support one side right from the start, but it also allows us to show that we have considered the other side of the debate but can explain why their reasons are not strong enough to win the argument.

On the other hand, if the arguments for both sides were quite equally balanced, then we might choose to do a compare/contrast essay in order to better explore both sides of the debate. However, it seems clear from the brainstorm that community work is largely beneficial for students, so we will write an argumentative essay to explain why we support it.

It is worth noting here that the essay prompt must always guide the type of essay that you write. If the prompt asks you to discuss the causes and solutions of a particular topic, then you must write about *only* the causes and solutions. If the prompt asks you to describe a process, then this is what you must do, and nothing else. If the prompt asks you to compare and contrast something in the past and the present, then you must do exactly this.

However, with questions that include phrases such as 'do you agree or disagree' or 'to what extent do you agree', there is more freedom to structure your essay in a way that best supports your opinion. If the facts are clear and there is no real debate, you might wish to write a cause/effect essay. If the evidence is 50/50 with good points on both sides, you might write a compare/contrast essay. If you agree 70%–90%, but you understand that there might be some validity to the other side of the debate, you might write an argumentative essay.

Based on the ideas from our brainstorm, we have decided to write an argumentative essay of five paragraphs in total in order to cover the most important information within an example time limit of 90 minutes and a minimum word count of 350. Now we have to decide which ideas to keep, which ideas to cut, and how to organize them.

Let's start with the introduction.

We need a hook first. We don't have access to the internet in this example, so we can't look for a quote or a statistic; therefore, we need to think of a good question or an observation about society that relates to the topic and will appeal to any reader no matter their age or background. Something about children or learning or helping others would be ideal as these things apply to everyone.

Next, we need background information (who, what, when, where, why, and how). We need to define what we mean by children participating in social work, who does it, what they do, where they do it, and why it is an important issue that is worth writing about.

Finally, we need to end the introduction paragraph with a thesis statement (preferably a direct thesis statement) that introduces an argumentative essay in support of the topic.

Now for the body paragraphs. Our brainstorm resulted in three potential paragraphs that support children participating in community work, but we only need two in order to meet the word-count requirement within the time limit. Therefore, we need to cut one. If we look back at our three categories, we have:

See the real world

- Learn outside school
- Have fun with friends
- Enjoy working with others
- Make new friends

Learn new skills

- Better communication skills
- Teamwork
- Keep our community clean
- Experience daily chores

Become more responsible

- Help less fortunate people
- Learn to care about others
- Learn from older generation
- Looks good on a resume

Considering the three main benefits, 'making friends' and 'having fun' seem the weakest, so we will cut these and focus on 'learning new skills' and 'becoming more responsible' for our two main supporting paragraphs. Of these two, learning new skills is probably the most obvious and happens quite quickly, so we will make this the first of the two supporting paragraphs. We will discuss becoming more responsible in the second supporting paragraph as this takes longer to occur, so it should logically come after skills development.

Now we need to look at the potential supporting ideas and improve these if necessary. Although we have decided to cut the first paragraph about making friends and having fun, 'see the real world' and 'learn outside school' could both be moved to the new skills paragraph and/or responsibility paragraph as they are strong valid arguments to support the activity.

In the skills paragraph, 'keep the community clean' is more of a result than a skill, so let's cut that and focus only on communication, teamwork, and chores.

In the responsibility paragraph, let's include 'seeing the real world' but cut 'learning from older generations' or our paragraph might become too long.

This leaves us with:

Learn new skills

- Better communication skills / teamwork
- Experience daily chores and tasks

Become more responsible

- See the real world
- Help less fortunate people
- Learn to care about others
- Looks good on a resume

Now that we have our two supporting paragraphs we need a counter-argument paragraph to demonstrate to the reader that we are aware of the other side of the debate and have considered their arguments.

To do this effectively, we must first of all introduce their main argument or arguments but in a way that then allows us to argue against them and explain why their opinion is wrong or at least not as strong as our opinion.

For a short essay, we will choose just one counter-argument — for this essay, dangerous. If you ask most parents what their biggest concern is about this activity, it is almost certainly the safety of their children, so we must address their concern head on and not ignore it. We must also explain their concern a little bit, but we should avoid making their point too strong.

Once we have introduced and explained the counter-argument, we then need to refute it (to explain why they are wrong or why our side of the argument is stronger than theirs). For example, if parents are worried about the safety of their children, we have to convince them that their children are actually very safe and explain why they are safe.

An outline for the counter-argument paragraph might look something like the following:

Counter-argument: Dangerous

- Working with strangers in a strange environment

Refutation: Not dangerous because

- Organized by professional teachers
- Supervised throughout
- Real-world environments are a vital part of learning

Putting it all together, we have the following outline for an argumentative essay on the topic of children being required to participate in community work as a part of their formal education:

Title: An Interesting Noun Phrase Related to the Topic

PARAGRAPH 1: Introduction

    Hook (question about helping others)

    Background about community service and volunteer work and about how some children do this as part of their school's education system

    Thesis statement in support of the topic with the two main reasons being skills development and a more mature attitude

PARAGRAPH 2: Supporting idea 1

    Learn new skills

        Better communication skills / teamwork

        Experience daily chores and tasks

PARAGRAPH 3: Supporting idea 2

    Become more responsible

        See the real world

        Help less fortunate people

        Learn to care about others

        Looks good on a resume

PARAGRAPH 4: Counter-argument + Refutation(s)

    Dangerous

        Working with strangers in a strange environment

    Not dangerous

        Organized by professional teachers

        Supervised throughout

        Real-world environments are a vital part of learning

PARAGRAPH 5: Conclusion

    Restatement of the main ideas

    Prediction about how this activity might affect children and society in the future

    A recommendation about how the reader or society as a whole might adjust to this issue

Now that we have an outline, we are ready to write our essay. If you would like to try, please write a 350-word argumentative essay about the value of community work using the outline above. Once you have finished your essay, compare your essay with the example essay on the next page.

3.7 Example argumentative essay: life lessons

Read the following example essay in the right-hand column. There is an explanation for each paragraph in the left-hand column.

Title: *An original title – not just stating the topic or copying the essay prompt.*	**Life Lessons**
Paragraph 1 **INTRODUCTION** *Hook: An interesting fact, quote, or question that grabs the reader's attention.* *Background info: Defines the issue and basic terms that the essay will discuss and answers the questions who, what, when, where, and why.* *Thesis statement: Both direct and indirect thesis statements are acceptable, but a direct thesis statement demonstrates a higher level of English language ability and also helps a reader to understand the structure and ideas of an essay.*	How often do you help others without expecting anything in return? Community service is voluntary work aimed at helping communities and individuals in need. Some people pursue this kind of work as a career, while others do it for free in their spare time. Additionally, many schools make their students participate in work such as this to develop their awareness of the world outside the classroom. Whether or not students should be required to participate in community service or not is a highly debatable issue. However, I believe that students should do community service because of the knowledge and responsibility that they obtain.
Paragraph 2 (BODY 1) **Supporting idea 1:** *Here, we deal with our first claim that students obtain knowledge and skills from community work. To support this, I explain that students learn (1) specific skills and the benefits they have, and (2) teamwork and the benefits of working with others. Both of these supporting points show the reader that students really do learn a lot by participating in community work (the main idea of the paragraph).*	First of all, children acquire knowledge and skills from community service work. One example of this is that organizers assign specific tasks and responsibilities for each participant. This means that kids learn how to do different jobs, but they can also see how their activities directly impact and improve the lives of those they are helping. Furthermore, community work involves team work. It is impossible for a single person to complete all the necessary tasks, so everything is assigned to teams. This means that students must work together to understand and successfully complete their assigned duties. Being able to coordinate and work together is a vital skill that can be difficult to teach and learn in a classroom. To sum up, children should participate in community work in order to develop their skills and abilities.

Chapter 3: Introduction to essays

Paragraph 3 (BODY 2)

Supporting paragraph 2:

This paragraph explains a totally different reason in support of our thesis statement — Students develop their sense of responsibility (not skills and abilities). To support this, I show that students understand (1) how lucky they are compared to others, (2) how they must behave with others, and (3) how this maturity and sense of responsibility will benefit them in the future. These supporting points help to persuade the reader that students really do become more responsible by participating in community work (the main idea of the paragraph).

Moreover, community service helps students to become more mature. One of the main reasons for this is that when students spend time helping those in need, they become more aware of the real world and more empathetic towards others. In other words, they see that other people are less fortunate than them, and this helps them to appreciate what they have. In addition, community service also teaches students to behave respectfully. That is, many students spend a lot of time watching and learning from the media, but forcing them to participate in their local community requires them to interact with people of different ages from different backgrounds in the real world. By doing this, they must consider their actions more carefully and adapt to different situations appropriately. Finally, companies nowadays increasingly want employees who also have compassion, and community work is a great to demonstrate this. Any resume is improved with evidence that an applicant has donated their free time to help others. Clearly, students can develop their character by participating in community service, and this will benefit them now and in the future.

Paragraph 4 (BODY 3)

Counter-argument and refutation paragraph:

Here, we address one idea that is opposite to ours, explained in a few different ways. I concede that there is a certain amount of truth to the opposing opinion, but I also go on to explain why they have misunderstood the issue. I provide a number of refutations in order to hopefully change their mind on this issue.

In spite of the aforementioned benefits, opponents argue that community service is not safe for children. They feel that children should be in school learning, not out in the community dealing with people and situations that they are unfamiliar with. At first glance, this argument may sound convincing. Nevertheless, these people overestimate the risk involved. School children are never required to work in dangerous situations. Moreover, the work involved is strictly organized and monitored and there are always teachers and other professionals working with them. Finally, taking children out of their insulated school environment is actually a vital part of their education as they need to experience real life and learn how to adapt.

Paragraph 5

CONCLUSION

Restates the thesis in fresh language and offers some meaningful reflection on how important community work is.

In summary, children should join community service as they will learn a lot and develop their character. Learning how to volunteer and interact with the real world at an early age is vital as kids are likely to grow up to be better people if they experience this valuable activity of helping others. As a result, I believe all schools should implement some form of community service as a part of their regular curriculum.

Complete the following reverse outline based on the previous essay *Life Lessons*. You do not need to use complete sentences. Just note form is okay in order to identify and note down the key points.

PARAGRAPH 1 (Introduction)

Hook:

_____

Background/linking information:

_____

_____

_____

Thesis statement:

_____

_____

PARAGRAPH 2 (Body paragraph 1)

Main idea of body 1 in support of the thesis statement:

_____

Supporting idea 1 + reason/explanation:

_____

_____

Supporting idea 2 + reason/explanation:

_____

_____

Supporting idea 3 + reason/explanation:

_____

_____

PARAGRAPH 3 (Body paragraph 2)

Main idea of body 2 in support of the thesis statement:

_____

Supporting idea 1 + reason/explanation:

_____

_____

Supporting idea 2 + reason/explanation:

_____

_____

Supporting idea 3 + reason/explanation:

_____

_____

PARAGRAPH 4 (Body paragraph 3)

Counter-argument against the main idea of the essay (against the thesis statement):

_____

_____

Refutation(s) (directly addressing opponents' counter-argument in order to change their mind):

_____

_____

_____

PARAGRAPH 5 (Conclusion)

_____

_____

3.8 Parallel structure

Now that we have discussed essay structure and development, let's look at some useful grammar. We will start with something that is essential for a direct thesis statement and many other aspects of writing — parallel structure. We already touched on this point in Chapter 1 when we dicussed a list of adjectives after a noun; for example, 'my dog is cute, fat, and old'. However, parallel structure causes countless errors and is worth covering in more detail in order to make your writing more accurate and effective.

Study the following example:

> International travel should be encouraged because of the opportunity to experience new cultures and the positive impacts on a person's character.

Do you see the parallel structure? 'Because of' is always followed by what? Look at the sentence again. In the example sentence above, the preposition 'because of' is always followed by nouns, so we have two nouns: the opportunity to experience new cultures (noun phrase #1) and the positive impacts on a person's character (noun phrase #2).

Parallel structure involves using the same pattern of language in order to show that two or more ideas are related to the same point and have the same level of importance. These ideas might be individual words, phrases, or even clauses. However, it is vital that they all be in the same form.

Study the following examples and notice how the word forms are parallel in the correct sentences:

| **(INCORRECT)** | Most teenagers enjoy relaxing, hanging out with friends, and surf the internet. |
| (CORRECT) | Most teenagers enjoy **relaxing**, **hanging** out with friends, and **surfing** the internet. |

In the example above, we need three gerund objects separated by commas with the conjunction '*and*' before the last in the list in order to create a grammatically correct simple sentence.

Let's look at another way that students sometimes create incorrect sentences due to a parallel structure error:

(INCORRECT)	Most teenagers enjoy relaxing, hanging out with friends, and they like to surf the internet.
(CORRECT BUT AWKWARD)	Most teenagers enjoy relaxing and hanging out with friends, and they like to surf the internet.
(CORRECT)	Most teenagers enjoy **relaxing**, **hanging** out with friends, and **surfing** the internet.

In this incorrect example, the writer has actually created a compound sentence, but this means that the first clause now has two objects (relaxing and hanging out with friends), which need to be separated with the conjunction 'and'. This results in a correct but awkward compound sentence. However, in English, it is almost always better to be concise and construct sentences that communicate a message using as few words as possible. As a result, the original correction using three gerund objects is much better.

Study the following sentences and label the parallel structure. The first one has been done for you as an example.

1. On weekends, I <u>do</u> my homework, <u>spend</u> time with my family, and <u>meet</u> my friends.
   (main verb — main verb — main verb)

2. When you write an essay, it is important to brainstorm ideas, to plan your essay, and to check it carefully.

3. When you write an essay, it is important to brainstorm ideas, plan your essay, and check it carefully.

4. At social events, you should dress appropriately, and speak politely and carefully.

5. More people obtain news from social media, such as Facebook and YouTube.

6. In the evenings and on weekends, I like to relax, play golf, and watch TV.

7. I believe that humans will eventually live in space and visit other planets.

8. My girlfriend told me what movie she wanted to watch and when we should meet.

9. My brother likes not only golf, but also football, tennis, and skiing.

10. Although it is not an easy decision, I recommend that students study for a master's degree due to the depth of knowledge and career opportunities that they can obtain.

3.9 Passive voice

Passive voice is used to show what happens (what *is done*) to someone or something, rather than what they do. Passive voice is used often by native speakers, especially in academic and scientific writing where the 'doer' is not necessarily important and the 'receiver' of the action, therefore, becomes the subject of the sentence. Passive voice should not be avoided just because it seems difficult. If you wish to become more fluent and skillful and get good scores on English tests and exams, you must become skillful with passive voice. Study the following:

Someone **stole my wallet**.   (Active sentence in which the subject of the sentence completes the action)

My wallet was stolen (by someone).   (Passive sentence in which the focus of attention is the missing wallet not the person who stole it)

The 'by' phrase is usually only included when it is important to know who performs/performed the action. All the verb tenses can be converted into passive voice although future continuous (will be being) and perfect continuous (has been being) are rare.

The following table shows how active tenses are converted into passive voice:

Tense	Active	Passive
Present simple	People make decisions	Decisions **are made**
Present cont.	People are making decisions	Decisions **are being made**
Present perfect	People have made decisions	Decisions **have been made**
Past simple	People made decisions	Decisions **were made**
Past continuous	People were making decisions	Decisions **were being made**
Past perfect	People had made decisions	Decisions **had been made**
Future simple	People will make decisions	Decisions **will be made**
Be going to	People are going to make decisions	Decisions **are going to be made**
Future perfect	People will have made decisions	Decisions **will have been made**

Note that intransitive verbs (verbs that are not followed by an object) cannot be used in the passive form because there is no object from the active sentence to use as the subject of a passive sentence. It is therefore not possible to use verbs such as *happen*, *disappear*, *die*, *fall*, and *seem* because *these verbs cannot be followed by an object*, so there is no object to use as the new subject of a passive sentence.

Compare the following:

(**INCORRECT**)   A man **was crashed** by a bus last night.
(CORRECT)   A man **was hit** by a bus last night.
(**INCORRECT**)   A man **was died** in the accident.
(CORRECT)   A man **was killed** in the accident.

Chapter 3: Introduction to essays

Change the following active sentences into passive *if possible*. However, be sure to keep the same verb tense and include the 'by' phrase only if it is appropriate.

1. People give presents every Christmas.

   _____

2. An accident happened outside my house last night.

   _____

3. People always tell me that I should go out more.

   _____

4. My dog usually sleeps at the end of my bed.

   _____

5. My father's company designed and built this house.

   _____

6. They are going to build a new hospital next year.

   _____

7. I spend most of my free time doing nothing useful.

   _____

8. Yesterday, the librarian put some new books in the library.

   _____

9. Scientists are making new discoveries in space all the time.

   _____

10. I waited an hour for my pizza.

    _____

Now let's try using passive voice in context. Complete the following sentences using active or passive in any appropriate tense for the verbs in parentheses.

1. Seventy percent of the earth's surface _____ (*cover*) by water, and ninety percent of the world's fresh water _____ (*lock*) in ice at the north and south poles.

2. Right now, my ten-year-old brother is in class. He _____ (*teach*) how to write an essay, but he _____ (*find*) English very difficult.

3. Students _____ (*allow*) to bring electronic devices into the classroom. However, Facebook, Instagram, and other social media should _____ (*avoid*) as they _____ (*distract*) students.

4. 65,000,000 years ago, an enormous asteroid _____ (*hit*) the earth and _____ (*kill*) the dinosaurs. The disappearance of the dinosaurs _____ (*allow*) mammals such as us to evolve.

5. The Second World War began when Poland _____ (*invade*) by Germany in 1939. The war only ended in Europe when Germany _____ (*beat*) by the Allies in 1945. Around 60,000,000 people from almost every nation on earth _____ (*die*) in WWII, but many positive developments _____ (*create*), including the United Nations, which _____ (*establish*) to protect human rights and prevent future wars.

3.10 Modal verbs

Modal verbs, or modal auxiliary verbs, such as *may, might, could, should, must,* and *will* are used before the infinitives of other verbs to add meaning connected with certainty or obligation or freedom to act. Modals are *not* usually used to say that something definitely exists or definitely happened. We use them to talk about things which we expect, which are not possible, which we want to happen, which we are not sure about, or which we think are necessary. Compare the following:

This *is* an academic writing textbook.	**FACT**
This *might be* an academic writing textbook.	**NOT SURE**
I *left* my homework in your car last night.	**FACT**
I *might have left* my homework in your car last night.	**NOT SURE**

Modal rules

1. Modals have no 's' in the third person singular.

    He **might wear** his uniform today (NOT He **might wears** his uniform today).

2. After modals, we use the base form of verbs.

    You **must do** your homework (NOT You **must to do** your homework).

3. Progressive, perfect, and passive verbs are also possible after a modal verb.

    He **might be working** on his assignment.

    She **shouldn't have copied** her homework.

    Graded work **cannot be written** at home.

4. '**Maybe**' should not be confused with '**may be**'. Although they have a similar meaning, '*maybe*' is an adverb, whereas '*may be*' is a modal verb followed by the base form of the verb 'to be', similar to 'might be'.

Compare the following:

   Maybe she is upstairs.

   She **may be** upstairs (She might be upstairs).

Adding tone

In argumentative essays, modals can be used to control the tone of your ideas. For example, words such as *must* and *should* show a reader what your opinion on a matter is. On the other hand, words such as *can, could, may, might, should* and *would* can be used to avoid making sweeping statements or to make an opposing opinion sound weaker.

Study the following example:

   While some people *may* say that uniforms don't help them get better grades, the evidence clearly shows that schools *should* enforce a strict uniform policy.

You are probably familiar with the basic uses of modals, but the following table contains a list of how modals can be used to more effectively communicate the certainty of an idea and your attitude towards it.

Modal	Uses	Past	Present	Future
may/might	less than 50% certainty	The government **may have changed** the school's uniform policy in yesterday's meeting. I know they were thinking about it, but I was absent yesterday, so I'm not sure.	There **may/ might be** a new uniform policy this year. We'll have to wait for the memo, but I'm sure they have decided.	There **may/might be** a new uniform policy next year. I know they're discussing it now, but we'll have to wait for a decision.
should	Advisability	The government **should have changed** its uniform policy years ago.	The government **should change** its uniform policy. The discipline problems are getting worse.	The government **should change** its uniform policy next year. The discipline problems will get worse if they don't.
must	a. strong necessity (note past tense form)	The government **had to drop** last year's new uniform policy because so many people complained.	The government **must introduce** a stricter uniform policy. The discipline problems are terrible.	The government **must introduce** a stricter uniform policy next year. The discipline problems will get worse if they don't.
	b. not allowed (negative)	X	Students **must not come** to class in jeans and T-shirts.	Students **must not come** to class in jeans next year. We weren't strict this year, but there will be a new policy soon.
	c. 95% certainty	The government **must have changed** its uniform policy recently. I didn't hear any news, but all the students are wearing different shirts.	There **must be** a new uniform policy. I didn't hear any news, but all the students are wearing different shirts.	The government **must change** its new uniform policy. Boys just don't look good in the new brown shirts.

Modal	Uses	Past	Present	Future
have to	a. necessity	The government **had to drop** last year's new uniform policy because so many people complained.	The government **has to introduce** a stricter uniform policy. The discipline problems are terrible.	The government **has to introduce** a stricter uniform policy next year. The discipline problems will get worse if they don't.
	b. lack of necessity (negative)	The government **didn't have to change** its uniform policy in yesterday's meeting. Everyone seems happy with the current policy.	The government **doesn't have to change** its uniform policy. Everyone seems happy with the current policy.	The government **doesn't have to change** its uniform policy in tomorrow's meeting. Everyone seems happy with the current policy.
will	100% certainty	X	X	The government **will change** its uniform policy tomorrow. I spoke to the prime minister this morning.
going to	a. 100% certainty (prediction)	X	X	Many students **aren't going to like** the new stricter uniform policy.
	b. definite plan (intention)	X	X	The government **is going to change** the uniform policy tomorrow. I spoke to the prime minister this morning.
	c. unfulfilled intention	The government **was going to change** its uniform policy yesterday, but many people complained, so they dropped the idea.	X	X
can	ability/ possibility	The government **couldn't decide** whether to introduce a new uniform policy or not yesterday.	The government **can't decide** whether to introduce a new uniform policy or not. They're still arguing about it.	X

Modal	Uses	Past	Present	Future
could	a. past ability	Students **could wear** anything they wanted to school in the past.	X	X
	b. suggestion	The government **could have chosen** a better color than brown for the new uniforms.	The government **could change** its policy if so many people are unhappy.	The government **could change** its policy in tomorrow's meeting if so many people are unhappy.
	c. less than 50% certainty	The government **could have changed** the school's uniform policy in yesterday's meeting. I know they were thinking about it, but I was absent yesterday, so I'm not sure.	There **could be** a new uniform policy this year. We'll have to wait for the announcement, but I'm sure they've decided.	There **could be** a new uniform policy next year. I know they're discussing it now, but we'll have to wait for a decision.
be able to	ability	The government **was able to reach** a decision yesterday. They will announce it today.	The government **is able to change** the uniform policy if it decides to.	The government **will be able to change** its policy if it doesn't work.
would	a. preference	The government **would have changed** the policy, but a lot of people complained, so they never did.	The government **would like** to change the uniform policy, but they are not sure what the public reaction will be.	The government **would like** to change the uniform policy next year, but they are not sure what the public reaction will be.
	b. unfulfilled wish	The government **would have changed** the policy, but a lot of people complained, so they never did.	X	X

Referring to the modal-verb rules in the previous tables, add an appropriate modal or phrasal modal to each verb in parentheses. More than one answer may be possible.

1. A lot of students (*skip*) _____ classes if teachers didn't take attendance.

2. John hasn't been to class all term, so he (*fail*) _____ next week's exam.

3. We (*go, not*) _____ to class today because it's a holiday.

4. I (*do*) _____ my homework last night, but I fell asleep.

5. Martin misunderstood what the teacher said in yesterday's English lesson, so he (*complete, not*) _____ the homework last night.

6. I told Sam we had an extra class today, but he (*misheard*) _____ me because he arrived one minute before the end of class and missed everything!

7. I feel terrible today! I knew that we (*go, not*) _____ to that party last night.

8. I (*leave*) _____ my book in the car. I had it this morning, but I can't remember what I did with it.

9. There (*be*) _____ another increase in fuel prices later this month if you believe the rumors.

10. The government (*do*) _____ more to fight corruption!

3.11 Avoiding weak connections

The idea of any essay is to prove that the main idea (the thesis statement) is true by providing factual and logical support. If you support your paragraphs with information and ideas that are *not* based on fact or reason, then the reader may not take your writing seriously. Therefore, there are a number of errors/weaknesses that you should avoid:

Sweeping statements

Bare collective nouns with no quantifier (such as *people* or *children* rather than *many people* or *most children*), quantifiers such as *all* and *every*, and adverbs such as *always* and *never* are often too general and can rarely be supported.

That doesn't mean you should avoid using these *types* of words completely, but other quantifiers such as *some, many, most* and other adverbs such as *rarely, sometimes,* and *often* give you the ability to show that you are aware that there may be exceptions to your statement and to grade your language accordingly.

You should be familiar with how to use these words in your writing, but it is important to stress their value in supporting a serious essay. You should be very careful of either not using an adverb or quantifier at all or using ones such as *all, every, always,* and *never* because your resulting sentence will be a sweeping statement that, unless you're sure it's true, could damage your argument.

Compare the following examples:

(**Sweeping Statement**)	People think religion is important.
(**Sweeping Statement**)	Everyone thinks religion is important.
(**Sweeping Statement**)	People always think religion is important.

The sentences above are sweeping statements that are clearly wrong because many people do not believe in a religion. Therefore, the impression of the essay as a whole has been damaged. Simply adding a more carefully chosen adverb or quantifier makes your sentence much more logical and believable and therefore much more likely to be taken seriously.

(CORRECT)	*Many* people think that religion is important.
(CORRECT)	People *might* think that religion is important.
(CORRECT)	People *often* think that religion is important.

Qualifying your statements with quantifiers, modals, and adverbs as in the examples above shows that you have considered other people's opinions and realize that there may be people who do not agree with the statement. Things are rarely true for *everyone*!

3.12 Using personal support

Specific support is good because you can give an example of what you are saying, but it is generally better to use factual *published* material as opposed to personal experience if you want your reader to take your essay seriously. Compare the following:

> (**INCORRECT**) My friend Chris goes to parties every night, but he still got an 'A' in his exam, so going to parties does not damage a student's education and I can party as much as I want.

Clearly, there is a problem with the logic of this reasoning, but it is also a good idea to stay away from using friends or relatives to support an essay unless it is a specific example of a more general supporting idea that has already been discussed.

> (CORRECT) A recent study by the Society of Technological Studies in Michigan found that 74% of students who went to parties regularly…actually did better on tests than those students who did not go out very often.

The example statistic above is made up (sorry), but do you see how much stronger it is as evidence for the point being made? Saying that something is true for one person does not mean it true for everyone or even most people. In fact, saying that something is true for one person is only evidence that is true for *one* person — no more.

You and I

In the same way that you should be careful of using friends and family as support, you should also be careful of using 'you' and 'I'.

First of all, using the pronoun '*you*' is referring directly to the reader, so you should be very sure of what you are saying to the reader before writing '*you*'. For example, if you write, 'If you go to study abroad, you can gain many valuable experiences', you have to remember that the reader of your essay has probably already graduated and, therefore, has no interest in going abroad to study. Therefore, it is not appropriate to say 'you'. Generally, as a rule, you should avoid saying 'you' in your essays.

Similarly, writing 'If I go to study abroad, I can gain many valuable experiences' makes it sound as though you are the only person to benefit, whereas you should be writing about students in general, not just yourself. 'If students go to study abroad, they can gain many valuable experiences' would be a much stronger sentence.

It should be noted, however, that if the essay prompt asks whether you agree or disagree with a particular issue, then you can give your opinion in the introduction and conclusion, but try to stick with objective evidence in the body paragraphs of your essay to prove that the main idea of your essay (your thesis statement) is true.

3.13 Logical fallacies

Most academic writing requires you to make an argument and present reasons and evidence for a particular claim. Organising and supporting your arguments is a very difficult skill that requires practice and patience — a bit like doing a jigsaw puzzle.

Fallacies are problems with logic that weaken arguments and damage an essay. By learning to look for them in your own and other people's writing, you can strengthen your ability to evaluate the arguments you make, read, and hear. It is important to realize two things about fallacies:

First, fallacious (faulty) arguments are very, very common and can be quite persuasive, at least to the casual reader or listener. You can find countless examples of fallacious reasoning in newspapers, advertisements, and other sources that try to persuade you into thinking or doing something.

Second, it is sometimes hard to evaluate whether an argument is fallacious, or not.

We will now introduce and discuss four of the most common logical fallacies to help you look critically at your own arguments and improve your logical development in order to write more persuasive essays.

Each argument you make is composed of a *premise* ((p) in the following examples) which is a statement that expresses your reasons or evidence to support your *conclusion* ((c) in the following examples) which is the main claim you are making. You can make your arguments stronger by:

1. Using good premises (ones you have good reason to believe are both true and relevant to the issue at hand).

2. Making sure your premises provide good support for your conclusion (and not some other conclusion, or no conclusion at all).

3. Addressing the most important or relevant aspects of the issue and not making claims that are so strong or sweeping that you can't really support them.

Chapter 3: Introduction to essays

The four most common problems that we see in student writing are presented on the following pages:

Circular argument

A circular argument occurs when the premise is the same as the conclusion. For example, "A is true because B is true, therefore B is true because A is true." This uses the circular reasoning fallacy. In other words, the support for an idea is simply that idea stated in a different way. The premise does not actually provide any support for the conclusion. Consider the following examples:

(**ILLOGICAL**)	He is not a good person (conclusion 'c') because he is a bad man (premise 'p').
(LOGICAL)	He is not a good person (c) because he lies often (p) and never helps others (p).
(**ILLOGICAL**)	Barack Obama is a good communicator (c) because he speaks effectively (p).
(LOGICAL)	Barack Obama is a good communicator (c) because he listens to others (p) and considers his responses carefully (p).

Slippery slope

In a slippery slope fallacy, you mistakenly argue against a proposal on the basis that it will inevitably lead to negative changes in the same direction. In other words, A will *definitely* lead to B and then C and D. This is also sometimes referred to as a snowball effect, domino effect or butterfly effect, but in this logical fallacy the ultimate effects are too far removed from the original event. In other words, you 'slip' down to an extreme conclusion based on incorrect assumptions. Consider the following examples:

(**ILLOGICAL**)	We should not legalize euthanasia (assisted suicide) (c). If we legalize it, more doctors will help their patients commit suicide (p), but then they will start killing patients who don't even want to die (p). Soon hospitals will become too dangerous for us to use (p).
(LOGICAL)	We should not legalize euthanasia (c). If we legalize it, **some** doctors will start helping their patients commit suicide (p), but **a few might even** kill patients who don't even want to die (p). ~~Soon hospitals will become too dangerous for us to use (p).~~
(**ILLOGICAL**)	We should not sell alcohol on university campuses (c). If we sell alcohol on campus, university students will start drinking when they study (p). Then high school students will start copying them (p), and pretty soon all the school children will become alcoholics (p).
(LOGICAL)	We should not sell alcohol on university campuses (c). If we sell alcohol on campus, **more** university students **might** start drinking ~~when they come to study~~ (p). Then **some** high school students **might** start copying them (p). ~~and pretty soon all the school children will become alcoholics (p).~~

99

Hasty generalization

Similar to the sweeping statements mentioned earlier in the chapter, a hasty generalization is when a general rule is created based on only a single or a few specific samples. This often occurs when people use their own limited experience to make judgments about something in general.

This is a fallacy because there is not enough evidence in the premise to draw any valid conclusions for a wider population.

Consider the following examples:

(ILLOGICAL)	The prime minister has lied countless times while in office (p). Therefore, you can't trust any politicians (c).
(LOGICAL)	The prime minister has lied countless times while in office (p). Therefore, we shouldn't trust him or vote for him next time (c).
(ILLOGICAL)	I used to own a Nokia, but I kept having problems with it (p), so it's clear that Nokia phones are terrible (c).
(LOGICAL)	I used to own a Nokia, but I kept having problems with it (p), so I've decided to try some other brands (c).

Appeal to authority

This is also known as 'Argument from Authority'. It occurs when a writer claims support from a particular person. An appeal to authority is often presented as "X is true because this person said so". However, the strength and message of the essay is damaged if the authority being used is not an expert in the field/subject being discussed.

On the other hand, there is also good appeal to authority when an author refers to the opinions or research of qualified and experienced experts in the field. In this case, it is logical to use their information to support your arguments. Therefore, there is good and bad appeal to authority, so you should always be careful to use reliable sources of information.

Consider the following examples:

(ILLOGICAL)	My cousin plays basketball and wears Nike Air (p), so they must be the best shoes for the sport (c).
(LOGICAL)	Michael Jordan always wore Nike Air (p), so they must be the best shoes for the sport (c).
(ILLOGICAL)	Dr. Jenkins, Dean of Faculty of Medicine at my university, said that we should invest in Tesla (p), so I'm going to invest some of my savings today (c).
(LOGICAL)	Dr. Jenkins, Chairperson of Business and Investment at my university and author of *Investment Know How*, said that we should invest in Tesla (p), so I'm going to invest some of my savings (c).

Chapter 3: Introduction to essays

Read the sentences below and decide if they are logical statements or if they are illogical for one of the fallacies we have just covered.

1. What do you think of these new CCTV video cameras around the city? To me, it seems like we should be really concerned with this new trend because it's something worth worrying about.

    A. Logical
    B. Slippery Slope
    C. Circular Argument
    D. Hasty Generalization

2. No human bones have ever been found in the same layer of rock as dinosaur bones. This is strong evidence that humans and dinosaurs never lived at the same time.

    A. Logical
    B. Slippery Slope
    C. Circular Argument
    D. Argument from Authority

3. I've met a few really nice people from Myanmar, so I think I'd like to live there as it's a really friendly and safe place to live.

    A. Logical
    B. Hasty Generalization
    C. Slippery Slope
    D. Circular Argument

4. Most Thai people do not speak English very well, so if an American tourist tried to talk to one or two random Thais, there would probably be communication problems.

    A. Logical
    B. Slippery Slope
    C. Circular Argument
    D. Argument from Authority

5. My laptop is much faster than my friend's desktop PC, so a laptop is definitely what you should buy if you want a high-speed computer.

    A. Logical
    B. Slippery Slope
    C. Hasty Generalization
    D. Circular Argument

6. Chinese characters are used in all the major languages of Northeast Asia. Japan is in Northeast Asia. This means that the Japanese language uses some Chinese characters.

    A. Logical

    B. Argument from Authority

    C. Slippery Slope

    D. Circular Argument

7. Oh, I did not know that. So you are saying that it is illegal for a taxi driver to refuse customers because the law says they can't?

    A. Logical

    B. Argument from Authority

    C. Slippery Slope

    D. Circular Argument

8. What about if people are motivated by the violent lyrics to commit violence, even kill, in real life? If more people here listened to his songs, the murder rate would surely go up. Eminem fans would soon be roaming around Bangkok attacking and murdering people.

    A. Logical

    B. Circular Argument

    C. Slippery Slope

    D. Hasty Generalization

9. The American government is trying to decrease the number of smokers. They've already raised taxes on cigarettes and banned smoking in many public places. Next, there will be a total smoking ban, and then they will ban other things that are bad for us like chocolate and soft drinks.

    A. Logical

    B. Argument from Authority

    C. Slippery Slope

    D. Circular Argument

10. Thailand is 95% Buddhist, so most Southeast Asian countries must be Buddhist.

    A. Logical

    B. Circular Argument

    C. Slippery Slope

    D. Hasty Generalization

3.14 Grammar check 3

Read the following argumentative essay and circle the correct answers. As you read for grammar, sentence structure, and word choice, also study the type of essay and the way in which it has been developed. Be prepared to explain your answers.

Growing (up, Up) Downtown

Growing up in (*an, the, Ø*) urban environment (*provide, provided, provides*) a very (*difference, different*) quality of life. Every (*parent wants, parents want*) the best for (*a, the, their*) family. (*As a result, On the other hand, So*) more and more people seek (*job, jobs*) opportunities and a better life in (*cities, city*). The (*quality, qualities*) of education and healthcare are two advantages that children (*obtain, will obtain*) if they live in (*the, a*) city.

The first obvious benefit is that (*most, most of*) children (*which, who, Ø*) grow up in cities (*will be, are, were*) provided a better education. One reason for (*it, this*) is that most (*city, city's, cities*) schools have many courses and (*facility, facilities*) that rural schools cannot provide. (*As a result, Nevertheless*), children can choose specific courses that they would like to study such as international business or computer programming. (*Consequently, In addition, However*), most (*teacher, teachers*) in urban schools have more (*experience, experiences*) and effective techniques, (*therefore, so*) students can learn more and obtain a better education. These educational advantages are one reason why growing up in (*the, a, Ø*) city is (*beneficial, benefit*) for every (*child, children, childrens*).

(*The another, Another*) reason to (*raise, raise up, grow up*) children in cities (*is, are*) that urban (*area, areas*) can provide effective healthcare services. One reason for this is that there (*is, are*) lots of (*hospital, hospitals*) (*provide healthcare, that provide healthcare*), which (*mean, means*) that children (*can easily, are easy to*) access (*to, Ø*) emergency medical treatments if they (*injure, are injured, injury*). With (*advanced, advance, advances*) medical (*equipment, equipments*) and expert (*doctor, doctors*) in most urban medical centers, (*so, and, Ø*) children (*are obtained, obtain, obtained, will obtain*) higher quality treatment. Clearly, better healthcare is (*available, availability*) for children in cities.

On the other (*hands, hand*), some (*parent, parents*) believe that raising children in cities (*obtains, results in*) a lower quality of life (*because of, because*) the higher cost of living. They argue that they have to spend (*money about 50% more, about 50% more money, money more than 50%*) on basic things such as food and accommodation. However, although their point may appear reasonable, (*but, Ø*) living in cities (*offer, offers*) more opportunities to find higher paying employment. This means that (*residence, residents, resident*) earn enough money to pay for not only their (*everyday, every day*) needs, but also superior education and healthcare for their family.

To conclude, raising children in cities (*obtains, provides*) a better lifestyle, and more children will obtain these benefits as (*a city, the city, city, cities*) grow.

3.15 Writing practice

Here are some ideas for you to practice writing argumentative essays. Look back at the model essays in this chapter for guidance and inspiration. Use the advantages and disadvantages table below to help you brainstorm arguments for both sides of each issue. There is also an outline for you to follow on the next page. Make sure you brainstorm and plan your essay first. This is essential for a well-organized and well-developed essay.

1. Do zoos still serve a useful purpose in today's world?
2. Should young children be allowed to own a smartphone?
3. Should teenage students be allowed to have part time jobs?
4. Is it important to travel and visit other countries, or not?
5. Should parents and teachers be very strict with children or allow them more freedom?
6. Should children be required to study extra classes in their free time?
7. Are social media such as Facebook and Instagram a positive influence on society?
8. As a student, is it better to live at home with family or in accommodation near university?
9. More children are growing up in cities these days. Is this a positive trend?
10. Should teenagers be allowed to date?

Topic to brainstorm	
Advantages	**Disadvantages**
1.	1.
2.	2.
3.	3.
4.	4.
5.	5.
6.	6.
7.	7.
8.	8.
9.	9.
10.	10.

3.16 Essay outline

Now group and support your ideas using the outline below to help you organize your ideas before you start to write an argumentative essay.

 There is a version of this outline available in the supporting online material.

PARAGRAPH 1 (Introduction)

Hook: _____

Background/linking information (who what when where why and how):

_____

_____

_____

Thesis statement:

_____

_____

PARAGRAPH 2 (Body paragraph 1)

Main idea of body 1 in support of the thesis statement:

_____

Supporting idea 1 + reason/explanation:

_____

_____

Supporting idea 2 + reason/explanation:

_____

_____

Supporting idea 3 (optional) + reason/explanation:

_____

_____

PARAGRAPH 3 (Body paragraph 2)

Main idea of body 2 in support of the thesis statement:

_____

Supporting idea 1 + reason/explanation:

_____

_____

Supporting idea 2 + reason/explanation:

_____

_____

Supporting idea 3 (optional) + reason/explanation:

_____

_____

PARAGRAPH 4 (Body paragraph 3)

Counter-argument against the main idea of the essay (against the thesis statement):

_____

_____

Refutation(s) (directly addressing the counter-argument in order to change their mind):

_____

_____

_____

PARAGRAPH 5 (Conclusion)

_____

_____

_____

3.17 Essay checklist

Once you have written your essay, use the following checklist to make sure you have all the correct components. If you answer 'yes' to all the questions below, well done!

1. Is there a correctly capitalized title (a noun phrase, *not* a statement or question)?

2. Is there an interesting hook related to the topic to grab the reader's attention?

3. Is there interesting and relevant background information (WWWWW+H)? What exactly is the topic? Why is this an important issue? How did this issue develop?

4. Is there a direct thesis statement that clearly states the main idea but also states the specific points that each supporting paragraph will discuss?

5. Does each body paragraph have a clear topic sentence introducing the main idea?

6. Does each paragraph have at least two different supporting ideas that relate to and support the main idea of the paragraph?

7. Do you sufficiently explain each supporting idea with relevant details and examples to help the reader fully understand each of the points you make?

8. Does every body paragraphs have a conclusion or at least end on a general statement? If a paragraph ends on quite a specific point, then it is nice to add a conclusion to remind the reader what big idea the paragraph is attempting to prove.

9. Are all of the paragraphs long enough? A good body paragraph should have a topic sentence, at least two supporting ideas (three better), explanations for each supporting point, and possibly a conclusion if necessary.

10. Is there a single clear counter-argument with a single *specific* reason against the main idea of the essay?

11. Does the writer acknowledge this counter-argument and effectively show why they are wrong and/or change their mind by addressing their concern?

12. Does the essay have a conclusion that restates the main points (not just copied from the thesis statement), and does the conclusion also include a prediction about the future or a recommendation for those affected by the issue?

13. Does the essay contain a good range of vocabulary and avoid repeating key words too much? Use Command/Control F to search for specific words and determine whether there is too much repetition, or not.

14. Is the essay correctly formatted according to your teacher's instructions?

15. Is punctuation correct throughout the essay, with capital letters only used at the start of each sentence and for all proper nouns?

16. Did you avoid saying 'you' and 'I' in your essay? You should never say 'you' as you do not know who will read your essay, and you should generally avoid saying 'I' unless the essay prompt asks for your opinion about something.

 Take the Chapter 3 Grammar Review in the supporting online material.

4. Using evidence

4.1 Discursive (compare/contrast) essays

In the previous chapter, you learned how to write an argumentative essay, where you brainstorm and choose a side before you start writing your essay. As part of an argumentative essay, you also include a counter-argument paragraph with a refutation to show that you have considered the other side of the argument, but you have stronger reasons to explain why the other side is wrong and hopefully change their mind about the issue.

In this chapter, however, you will write a discursive essay, in which you will not decide which side of the debate you support until the conclusion. What this means is that you will essentially describe the arguments for both sides (i.e. one paragraph for the supporting arguments and one paragraph for all the opposing arguments), and then in the conclusion you will explain which side you agree with (if any), and why, based on the arguments that you put forward in the body paragraphs. Essentially, it is a compare/contrast essay that leads to a logical conclusion of some kind at the end.

Many students think a discursive essay is easier because they only need to write four paragraphs (in the most basic block-method compare/contrast essay), but in some ways this essay is harder because you must be careful to cover all the main benefits and drawbacks, sometimes comparing and contrasting within each paragraph, too. If you forget to include an important aspect of the issue or you fail to explain its significance in relation to the topic of the essay and the alternatives available, it can severely damage the overall quality and perception of your essay.

In addition, once we have covered the basic essay structure and some useful grammar to help you develop your ideas, we will also introduce the important concept of using evidence to support your ideas. Using evidence correctly in an academic essay is no easy task, but we will explain the basic rules and practice through structured exercises before you then find and use your own evidence to support your essays.

If we don't have evidence to support our ideas, people are less likely to believe us and agree with us, but, perhaps more importantly, if we don't have evidence to support our ideas, maybe we are wrong to think that!

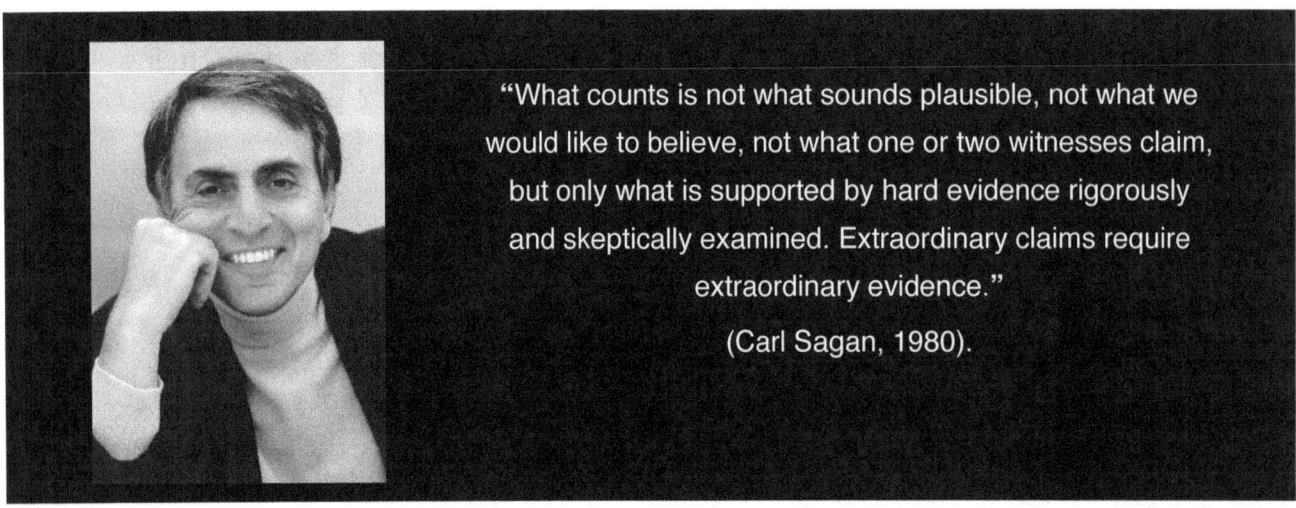

"What counts is not what sounds plausible, not what we would like to believe, not what one or two witnesses claim, but only what is supported by hard evidence rigorously and skeptically examined. Extraordinary claims require extraordinary evidence."

(Carl Sagan, 1980).

Read the following discursive essay and then complete the reverse outline that comes after. As you read, think carefully about how the essay has been organized and supported. Notice how it differs from an argumentative essay.

After-Class Hell

What should children really learn? On top of my regular school hours, signing up for additional classes in the evenings and weekends when I was a child would have felt like a terrible punishment. However, it is quite common these days, especially in Asia, for children and young adults to take many hours of extra tuition throughout their education. Learning is always a worthwhile goal, but there are different ways to obtain a good quality, well-rounded education. This essay will discuss the positive and negative aspects of regularly taking extra classes in order to then determine how valuable this common practice really is.

The beneficial aspects of taking extra classes are quite straightforward. First of all, a student simply learns more. Whether it be skills, knowledge, or values, spending time learning with a tutor will increase what one knows and can do because they can ask more questions and get more practice. Knowing more about science, for example, will open doors to understanding our place in the physical world and how it operates. The second advantage is that extra classes increase students' GPA scores, which ensures acceptance into better universities and better careers in the future. Private tutors often have better information and practice exercises than schools provide. This results in more knowledge and higher grades, increasing a student's quality of life.

On the other hand, spending a large amount of time studying extra classes presents drawbacks. First of all, the lack of relaxation and sleep can have a terrible impact on a young person's state of mind. Working 8, 10, or even 12 hours a day would be hard for anyone, and countries where this is common have higher rates of childhood depression and suicide than other countries. In addition, gaining knowledge only from books and tutors is not the only way to learn. People should experience the world in a variety of contexts to develop a well-rounded knowledge of the world. Memorizing information in textbooks does not allow for the application of that knowledge in the real world. Reading about building a business and actually attempting to build a business are very different. Furthermore, gaining knowledge outside of the classroom allows for a wider range of equally healthy pursuits such as exercise, constructive hobbies, and interaction with people from different walks of life. For instance, volunteering in one's local community, taking a part-time job, or joining a sports club offer more opportunities to grow and develop.

Considering both sides of this debate, it is my opinion that taking many extra classes is too restrictive, despite the potential advantages. It may be useful or necessary in some cases to hire a tutor, but children should spend their evenings and weekends taking advantage of more dynamic opportunities to learn and mature. There are any number of options in this regard. They might join a play, go camping, help out in their community, tutor a younger child, or learn to study independently. Whichever they choose, the motivation and sense of responsibility they learn from these activities will serve them well for years to come, in ways that extra classes simply can't achieve.

Complete the following reverse outline based on the previous essay *After-Class Hell*. You don't need to copy whole sentences.

The point of this exercise is to carefully consider and understand how the essay has been organized and developed.

PARAGRAPH 1 (Introduction)

Hook: _____

_____

Background/linking information (who what when where why + how):

_____

_____

_____

Thesis statement: _____

_____

PARAGRAPH 2 (Body paragraph 1)

Main idea of the paragraph:

_____

Supporting idea 1: _____

Reason/evidence for supporting idea 1:

_____

_____

Supporting idea 2: _____

Reason/evidence for supporting idea 2:

_____

_____

Chapter 4: Using evidence

Supporting idea 3: _____

Reason/evidence for supporting idea 3:

_____

_____

PARAGRAPH 3 (Body paragraph 2)

Main idea of the paragraph:

_____

Supporting idea 1: _____

Reason/evidence for supporting idea 1:

_____

_____

Supporting idea 2: _____

Reason/evidence for supporting idea 2:

_____

_____

Supporting idea 3: _____

Reason/evidence for supporting idea 3:

_____

_____

PARAGRAPH 4 (Conclusion)

_____

_____

4.2 Present perfect

Read the following paragraph and underline all the main verbs. Be prepared to discuss why the different verb tenses were used and the difference in meaning in each case.

A New Beginning

People have always <u>dreamed</u> of traveling into space and exploring other planets, and we are now closer than ever to making that dream a reality. NASA and other space agencies have worked on projects to send satellites and robotic rovers to explore Mars for decades, and SpaceX has made amazing progress on its own project to explore space and inhabit other planets. NASA's two newest rovers, Curiosity and Perseverance, have provided a goldmine of information that will help us eventually send a manned mission to the red planet and eventually other planets that are orbiting other stars. Humans haven't left low-earth orbit since the moon landings of the 1960s and 70s, but that will soon change. The success of humanity's recent missions to Mars has widened our view of what is possible and set new standards for cooperation between people back here on Earth. 'Hope' has been given new meaning.

Chapter 4: Using evidence

The perfect tenses are extremely hard for non-native speakers to fully understand and use correctly, especially if there is no equivalent in your native language. You first *learned* the simple tenses (past tense), and you *are now studying* present perfect (present continuous tense).

You *know* a lot of grammar (present simple), and you *have certainly studied* present perfect before (present perfect), but you *have probably forgotten* most of the rules (present perfect), so we *will briefly study* present perfect again (future tense).

Read the paragraph on the previous page again and think about the time frame each sentence is referring to. The following explanations and exercises should help you to better understand present perfect verb forms and how to use them more accurately in your writing.

Present perfect simple		
TIMELINE	**FUNCTION**	**EXAMPLE**
PAST PRESENT FUTURE	The present perfect can express the idea that something happened (or never happened) at an *unspecified time in the past*. The exact time it happened is not important and not specified (a, b, c). Conversely, when referring to a specific time in the past, the simple past is used (d, e).	(a) I **have been** to America. (b) You **have studied** present perfect before. (c) We **have never visited** your uncle. (d) I **went** to Rio **last year**. (e) My father **started** his own business **in 1974**.
PAST PRESENT FUTURE	Present perfect can also be used to say that a finished event is connected to the present in some way. If we say that something *has happened*, we are thinking about the past and the present at the same time, and there is often a result *now* (a, b, c). *'Just'* can also be added to a perfect sentence to express a completed action that happened *very* recently (d).	(a) My sister **has broken** her leg. She can't walk. (b) Our dogs **have disappeared**. We can't find them anywhere. (c) It **has stopped** raining. It was raining, but now the sun is shining. (d) I **have just spilled** the milk. It's all over the floor.
PAST PRESENT FUTURE	We can also use present perfect to say that something has happened a number of times up to now, but the exact time of each action is not important or stated.	(a) I **have drunk** three cups of coffee today. (b) I **have seen** Mission Impossible three times. (c) We **have made** many new friends since last week.

Read the following situations and write sentences using the verb in parentheses in the present perfect tense.

1. Last month, Lucy had a Toyota. Now she has a Mercedes. (*buy*)

    Example answer: Lucy has bought a Mercedes.

2. A friend gives you a DVD to watch. You already have the movie at home. (*see*)

3. John was here five minutes ago. Now, he is not here. (*go*)

4. My father smoked for twenty years. Now, he does not smoke. (*quit*)

People have always mixed up our names!

Chapter 4: Using evidence

Present perfect progressive

TIMELINE	FUNCTION	EXAMPLE
PAST PRESENT FUTURE	Present perfect progressive is commonly used to indicate the duration of an activity that *began in the past and continues to the present*. The important difference between present perfect simple and progressive is that perfect progressive has more of an '*up to now*' focus. It is common when we are talking about how long a situation has lasted, or when we are talking about a situation that is just coming to an end or may change. When used in this way, it is often followed by time words such as *since*, *for*, *all day*, and *all year*. **Note:** With certain verbs such as *live*, *work*, *study*, and *teach*, the present perfect simple or continuous can both be used with no difference in meaning (d, e).	(a) I **have been sitting** here since eight o'clock. (b) It **has been raining** all morning. (c) I **have been working** for three hours, but I need a break, so I'll stop. (d) My brother **has lived** in England since he was a child. (e) My brother **has been living** in England since he was a child.
PAST PRESENT FUTURE	Both the present perfect tenses (simple and progressive) can be used to talk about recent actions and situations that have results in the present. The important difference is that the progressive form focuses on the activity itself, but the simple form focuses on the result.	(a) I **have been reading** all morning. (focus on activity) I **have read** both books you gave me. (focus on result) (b) The professor **has been lecturing** for two hours, and he still **has not finished**. (focus on activity followed by result) The professor **has lectured** for three hours, so we can go home now. (focus on result)

115

Read the following situations and write sentences using the verb in parentheses in the present perfect progressive tense.

1. It started raining at 8 o'clock. It is now 10 o'clock and it is still raining. (*rain*)

   Example answer: It **has been raining** since 8 o'clock, or it **has been raining** for two hours!

2. You started learning English when you were six. You are still learning. (*learn*)

   _____

3. You meet a friend of yours. He has a black eye and a bloody nose. (*fight*)

   _____

4. Your aunt is making dinner. She started cooking at 10am, but it is now 1pm. (*cook*)

   _____

We have been studying grammar for an hour. Please stop!

Chapter 4: Using evidence

Now that you have a better understanding of the different tenses in English, complete the following sentences with any appropriate tense: past simple, past progressive, past passive, past perfect, present simple, present progressive, present passive, present perfect, present perfect progressive, future simple, or future progressive.

1. I (*not, swim*) _____ in the sea since I saw the shark movie *Jaws*.

2. Thailand (*have*) _____ one of the highest average temperatures in the world.

3. My brother is usually lazy, but he (*work*) _____ hard at the moment because he (*save*) _____ money for a new car.

4. Many people (*say*) _____ that marijuana should (*legalize*) _____.

5. Don't call me tomorrow morning because I (*study*) _____.

6. We (*study*) _____ present perfect for the last 30 minutes, but we still (*not, finish*) _____!

7. Right now, everyone (*do*) _____ English grammar exercises. Most of us (*study*) _____ verb tenses before, but English grammar (*always, be*) _____ difficult.

8. I (*not, see*) _____ a good movie for ages. I (*find*) _____ one interesting movie to watch last night, but just as we (*sit*) _____ down to watch it, my wife's mother (*call*) _____!

9. Since the beginning of this writing course, we (*study*) _____ grammar in every writing class. Right now, we (*study*) _____ present perfect. At the start of class today, our teacher (*explain*) _____ it to us, and we (*try*) _____ to understand it for the last hour.

10. My father (*write*) _____ his memoir for the last three years! He (*publish*) _____ one other book about 5 years ago, but it (*not, sell*) _____ very well, so he (*put*) _____ a lot of time and effort into this one to make sure it is good.

117

4.3 Gerunds and infinitives

Another point that causes countless errors in student writing is the difference between a gerund and an infinitive and when to use them. A gerund is a noun made from a verb by adding '~ing'. The gerund form of the verb 'read' is 'reading' (For example: I like reading, so reading is my hobby.). You can use a gerund in the same way that you can use any noun. However, not every '~ing' word is a gerund. Compare the following:

Walking is good for you. (gerund noun as the subject of the sentence)

My hobby is **walking** in the countryside. (gerund noun as the object of the sentence)

I am interested in **walking** in the countryside. (gerund noun as the object of the preposition)

My dog is **walking** into the house. (present continuous main verb)

My mother needs a **walking** stick these days. (participle adjective describing the stick)

Gerunds	
FUNCTION	**EXAMPLE**
A gerund can be used as the subject(s) of a sentence.	**Swimming** is good for you. **Watching** TV and **playing** video games are bad for your eyes.
A gerund can be used as the object(s) of a verb.	We enjoy **studying** grammar. We don't mind **working** hard and **doing** our homework
A gerund can also be used as the object of a preposition.	I am interested **in studying** business. They are talking **about going out** tonight.
Some verbs can be followed by object + gerund.	I **appreciate you helping** me. It's important to **spend time reading**.
A negative gerund is made by simply adding *not* before the gerund.	I always deny **not doing** my homework.

Remember that ~ing forms can also be used in the present progressive (e.g. I *am working*) or as an adjective (e.g. That is an *interesting* book).

Common verbs followed by gerunds			
appreciate	endure	can't help	practice
avoid	enjoy	imagine	resent
consider	(can't) face	involve	resist
delay	feel like (= want)	keep (on)	risk
deny	finish	mention	suggest

Infinitives, such as (to) read and (to) write are used to refer to actions and events in a general way. They do not usually express when events happen, so they should not be confused with verb tenses. Infinitives have many functions and rules. Study the following:

Infinitives	
FUNCTION	**EXAMPLE**
A bare infinitive (without *to*) is used after the modals *will*, *would*, *should*, *may*, *might*, *can*, *could*, and *must* as part of a verb phrase.	You **must work** harder! Everyone **should listen** to their parents.
An infinitive can be used as the subject or complement of a clause, but a gerund is much more common as the subject of a sentence.	**To write** well is difficult. (infinitive subject) **Writing** well is difficult. (gerund subject) It is important **to practice**.
An infinitive can be used to express a person's purpose (the reason for doing something).	I work hard **to earn** money (in order to earn money). Mark went home **to study** (in order to study).
A negative infinitive is made by simply adding *not* before the infinitive.	Try **not to wake up** late tomorrow! It is important **not to skip** class.
Some verbs such as *let*, *make*, *see*, *hear*, *feel*, *watch*, and *notice*, are followed by an object + bare infinitive (without *to*).	My mother **made me clean** the car. I **heard you say** my name. She **let me drive** her car!
When two infinitive verbs are joined by *and*, *or*, *but*, *except*, *than*, *as*, or *like*, the second infinitive is usually used without *to*.	I like **to read** and **watch** TV. There was nothing **to do** except **watch** the rain.

Common verbs followed by infinitives			
afford	continue	hope	pretend
agree	dare	intend	promise
appear	decide	learn	refuse
arrange	expect	like	remember
ask	fail	love	seem
attempt	forget	manage	start
begin	hate	offer	try
care	help	prefer	want
choose	hesitate	prepare	
For example: You **forgot to submit** your homework again! My father **promised to buy** me a new phone if I get good grades.			

Common verbs followed by object + infinitve			
advise*	expect	like	recommend*
allow*	forbid*	love	remind
ask	force	need	teach
cause	help*	order	tell
encourage*	invite	persuade	want
For example: Mrs. Jones **encouraged me to practice** reading more often. My brother **needs me to help** him with his homework.			
Note: *Advise, allow*, and similar words can often be followed by an ~ing form if there is no object. If there is an object, we use an infinitive. For example: She **advised taking** an extra class. She **advised me to take** an extra class.			

Some verbs can be followed by either a gerund or an infinitive with no difference in meaning.

Infinitive of gerund with no difference in meaning			
begin	hate	love	start
continue	like	prefer	try
For example: Jimmy **hates to do** his homework / Jimmy **hates doing** his homework. I **prefer to watch** movies at the cinema / I **prefer watching** movies at the cinema.			

However, other verbs can be followed by either a gerund or an infinitive, but the meanings are different. Compare the following:

Infinitive of gerund with a difference in meaning	
INFINITIVE OR GERUND?	EXAMPLE
(a) **Remember/forget doing** something refers back to something that happened in the past, but **remember/forget to do** something refers to a task or responsibility	I **remember locking** the door, so why is it open? I must be more careful and **remember to lock** the door before I go out in the future.
(b) To **Stop doing** something means to discontinue an activity. On the other hand, to **stop to do** something means to discontinue one activity in order to do something else.	I will never **forget seeing** my first rock concert, but I keep **forgetting to buy** tickets for us to see one together. My father **stopped smoking** years ago, but I saw him **stop to buy** a pack of cigarettes yesterday!

Complete the following sentences with an infinitive or a gerund.

1. Our math teacher told us _____ (*bring, not*) our calculators tomorrow!

2. Now that I am old, I miss _____ (*be*) young.

3. In the future, I hope _____ (*own*) my own business.

4. My mother always warns me _____ (*talk, not*) to strangers.

5. People who live in apartment buildings are not allowed _____ (*keep*) pets or _____ (*have*) guests after 11pm.

6. My friends talked about _____ (*go*) on holiday together at the end of term, but they decided _____ (*have*) a party at my house instead of _____ (*spend*) too much money on an expensive vacation.

7. _____ (*help*) people is a good thing to do because other people might not be as lucky as us, and it makes you _____ (*feel*) good.

8. _____ (*talk*) to native speakers encourages me _____ (*speak*) more English and _____ (*practice*) my skills. I sometimes avoid _____ (*talk*) in English because I get embarrassed, but I know I need _____ (*keep*) _____ (*try*) so that I will improve.

9. I usually finish _____ (*write*) my assignments early, but I know I should read them again _____ (*check*) for mistakes.

10. _____ (*know*) how to use a computer is very useful. I can practice _____ (*read*) and _____ (*write*). This helps me _____ (*improve*) my skills and _____ (*learn*) more!

4.4 Using evidence

Now that we have introduced a new type of essay and some useful grammar for you to use, we will move on the main focus of this chapter — using evidence to support your writing. The information in brackets, such as (Smith, 2014), is called a citation and we use these in academic writing to show the reader where we obtained our information. To start with, study the following example paragraphs and consider what is good or bad about them. Which of the three paragraphs is better and why?

While Japan is the world leader for environmental protection, this has not always been the case. In the past, Japan recycled very little of its waste, but today it is famous for recycling most of it, and there are lots of news stories about the Japanese separating waste into many different bins and being very efficient with the natural resources that the country consumes (Ikuro, 2014). This is because, as everyone knows, Japan is a relatively small country, and it doesn't have sufficient natural resources to supply the whole country with what people need, so the government encourages people to recycle more and waste less (WHO, 2014). As a result, Japan now consumes fewer natural resources and produces less pollution because it recycles so much waste.

While Japan is the world leader for environmental protection, this has not always been the case. The country recycled less than 30% of plastic waste in 1986 compared to the current figure of just over 75% (Ikuro, 2014). There are several laws that require businesses and consumers to separate plastic waste have been brought into effect since 1997 ("Japan recycles", 2015). According to the WHO (2014), the government introduced a series of public service advertisements that explain the benefits of separating out plastic. Japan now consumes fewer natural resources and produces less pollution because it recycles so much waste.

While Japan is the world leader for environmental protection, this has not always been the case. One aspect that the country has focused on is recycling. According to Dr. Arai Ikuro (2014), head of environmental studies at Tokyo University, the country recycled less than 30% of plastic waste in 1986 compared to the current figure of just over 75%. This is important because it means the country needs fewer natural resources and produces less pollution from waste disposal or the manufacture of new products. This change has come about partly as a result of legislation and partly from a clearly focused educational program. For example, several laws that require businesses and consumers to separate plastic waste have been brought into effect since 1997 ("Japan recycles", 2015), and those measures have been supplemented with a series of public service advertisements that explain the benefits of separating out plastic (WHO, 2014). This means that people are forced to recycle more, but they also understand the value in doing this. As a result, Japan now consumes fewer natural resources and produces less pollution because it recycles so much waste.

4.5 Citations and references

Part of the academic writing process is using evidence to support your essays. One of the most important aspects of academic writing is using documented facts and the opinions of experts. This is important because you need to show that you have understood the subject that you have studied and that you can use expert opinions and research to support your own ideas on the subject. In fact, this is an essential skill for every student.

In other words, the object of academic writing is for you to present your ideas in your own way, but to help you do this, you use information and ideas from other people to support your points. However, when you do this, you *must* say where the facts and opinions were obtained.

It will always be assumed that the words or ideas are your own if you do not say otherwise. Therefore, when the words or ideas you are using are taken from another writer, and are obviously not general knowledge, you must make this clear by citing your sources. If you do not do this and use another person's research and opinions as if they were your own, this is plagiarism, and plagiarism is regarded as a very serious offence.

There are many ways of referring to your sources of information, but we will focus on the American Psychological Association (APA) style, which is well known and widely used around the world, especially in social sciences and business.

Citing and referencing your sources can be extremely complex, but it has to be in order to cover all the possible ways in which a writer might obtain information. However, please follow the basic rules described here.

There are two ways in which you can use another person's work: paraphrasing or "quoting". Paraphrasing simply means reporting another person's information and ideas in your own words. Paraphrasing is generally used when the exact wording is not important. When the wording *is* important, it is often better to quote the expert using their exact words in "quotation marks". As a result, we generally only quote expert opinions and official definitions as both of these are usually worded extremely carefully in order to convey precise meaning.

If you do decide to quote someone, keep the quotation as brief as possible and quote only when it is necessary. You must always have a good reason for using a quote. Feeling unable to paraphrase or summarize is never a good reason.

The idea of an essay is for you to communicate ideas that you have developed and information you have obtained and analyzed in your own way. The emphasis should be on working *with* other people's ideas, not reproducing their words. Your paper should include information from various sources, expressed in your own words, not a collection of quotations. Any quote you use should add something to the point you are making.

4.6 Facts and opinions

When you research a topic, you need to decide if the evidence is an opinion or a fact. If it is a fact, then it should be paraphrased as the wording will not be as important as the information. On the other hand, if it is the opinion of an expert or an internationally accepted definition of something, then the words will be very carefully chosen in order to precisely convey exact meaning. In this instance, with a carefully worded statement of opinion or a carefully worded definition of something, you should quote in order to retain the exact meaning of the original sentence. However, you should not quote too much!

Reasons for *not* using quotations include the following:

1. Do not quote if the information is already well-known.
2. Do not use a quotation that disagrees with you unless you plan to argue against them and prove that the quoted statement is wrong.
3. Do not quote if you cannot understand the meaning of the original sentence.
4. Do not quote just because you don't feel able to paraphrase the original sentence.
5. Do not use quotations to make your points for you; use them to support your points.

One difficulty that students encounter is differentiating fact from opinion and then determining which opinions should be quoted. Label the following sentences F for facts and O for opinions. Put quote marks (" ") around the sentence(s) that you think should be quoted. Remember, we usually quote somebody if their statement is very carefully worded in order to convey exact meaning or an important message. We do not usually quote general knowledge or statements where the wording is not particularly important. Be prepared to discuss your choices.

A. _____ The functionality of smartphones has made daily life easier.

B. _____ 75% of 13–18-year-olds own a smartphone.

C. _____ People are prisoners of their phones, which is why we call them **cell**phones.

Now try the same exercise but with five sentences.

1. _____ Although his critics called him a socialist, President Franklin D. Roosevelt's policies saved the economy from bankruptcy.

2. _____ President Franklin D. Roosevelt (FDR) initiated New Deal policies that provided more employment opportunities for the working class.

3. _____ Franklin D. Roosevelt once said that the only thing we have to fear is fear itself.

4. _____ Biographer Robert Dallek believes that no other leader has commanded as much respect as Roosevelt.

5. _____ In his first 100 days as president, FDR introduced a range of new legislation that was designed to regulate private industry and the banks.

4.7 How to cite and reference

Whether you decide to paraphrase or use a quotation, you must be very careful to make it clear that the information and opinions that you are using are taken from another writer. You need a *citation* (even if you have paraphrased the information) in order to show the reader where the information came from. This can be done in several ways, all of which are correct. Compare the following examples of different but equally acceptable quotes and paraphrases with accompanying citations:

QUOTE:	Widdowson (1979) states, "Learning is the foundation of civilization."
PARAPHRASE:	Widdowson (1979) states that civilization is built on education.
QUOTE:	According to Harold Widdowson (1979), "Learning is the foundation of civilization."
PARAPHRASE:	According to Harold Widdowson (1979), civilization is built on education.
QUOTE:	According to one researcher, "Learning is the foundation of civilization" (Widdowson, 1979).
PARAPHRASE:	According to one researcher, civilization is built on education (Widdowson, 1979).

In academic writing, we include a citation like the Widdowson examples above to acknowledge that the information comes from someone else and to give the reader an indication of the source used. Academic essays should be full of evidence from different sources in support of the different ideas and arguments that are presented. As a result, academic essays are also full of citations with each piece of evidence in order to credit the original source and enable the reader to check the information if they wish to.

However, the information in a citation (the family name and date in most cases) is not sufficient on its own because there may be many authors of that name who published in a certain year, and the reader would probably not be able to find the exact same source with just the family name and year. Therefore, at the end of every essay, we have a references page, where all the detailed information for each source is provided. Therefore, for every citation in the body of the essay, there is a matching reference at the end of the essay. If a reader has questions or doubts about some of the evidence that they see in your essay, they can look at the citation and then find the matching reference at the end of the essay (with all the detailed information) so that they can visit the same original source as you and check that you interpreted and used the evidence correctly. This is the point of academic writing — to research and analyze current knowledge from respected sources and then add your own interpretations, research, conclusions, and opinions to the topic.

The reference for the example citations in the table above might look something like this:

> Widdowson, H. G. (2013). *Explorations of human civilizations through time.* Oxford: Oxford University Press.

A standard APA reference follows the format:

> Family Name, Initial(s). (Year, Month Date). Title of the article. Name of the Organization. URL or Other Source Location Information

The example citations and the corresponding reference on the previous page all assume, however, that you have the author and date, and that you used a book! This is not always the case, and articles often appear with no author, no date, or neither, especially on the internet!

If this happens, there is a series of steps that you must go through in order to determine the correct citation and matching reference for a particular source.

The table on the next page explains the rules in order of preference, but note that a standard reference where the author and date are known follow this order: the author's family name and first initial(s), followed by the date (year, month date), followed by the title of the webpage or article (with just the first word and any proper nouns capitalized), followed by the name of the organization (correctly capitalized as a proper noun), followed by the web address if it was retrieved online (APA 7 no longer requires the 'Retrieved from…' phrase, so just include the web address URL link on its own).

Confused?

If you are, you are not alone.

Correctly crediting sources is extremely complex due to the variety of sources available, but this is an essential skill as a professional student and definitely something that you will need to know in order to write effective college and professional papers.

In fact, in today's world, one could argue that critically analyzing information is perhaps more important than ever before in all walks of life, so please pay careful attention as you work through this chapter.

If confusion indicates learning, I must be a genius!

This table explains how to cite a source given varying amounts of source information.

OPTION 1: Webpage with author	**Citation in the body of your essay:** (Smith, 2009), or According to Dr. Gary Smith (2009), or Dr. Gary Smith (2009) states that... **Reference at the end of your essay:** Smith, G. (2009). An introduction to behavioral approaches. *Counseling Resources.* http:/counsellingresource.com/types/ **Note:** The reference includes the author's family name and first initial (in that order), followed by the date (year, month date), the title of the webpage, the name of the organization, and the source URL.
OPTION 2: Webpage with no individual author but it is a well-known international corporate author	**Citation in the body of your essay:** (National Defense Department, 2004) or According to Canada's National Defense Department (2004), etc. **Reference at the end of your essay:** National Defense Department. (2004). Post-traumatic stress disorder. http://www.forces.gc.ca/site/news-nouvelles
OPTION 3: Webpage with no author or well-known corporate author or a webpage from a news agency	**Citation in the body of your essay:** ("Nurses of the 21st century," 2006) **Reference at the end of your essay:** Nurses of the 21st century are finding it harder than ever to find work. (2006). http:/secure.cihi.ca/cihiweb/NHSRep06.pdf **Note:** We use a shortened title for the in-text citation if the title is very long. In addition, we put the title in quotation marks and only capitalize the first word to show the reader that this is not a person's name.

NO DATE:
 	
Any of the above but with no date, so replace the year (2006) with no date (n.d.)
	Citation in the body of your essay:
	(Shields, n.d.), or According to Dr. David Shields (n.d.), or Dr. David Shields (n.d.) states that...
	
	Reference at the end of your essay:
	Shields, M. (n.d.). *Findings from the National Survey of Nurse*s.
	    Canadian Institute for Health Information.
	    http:/secure.cihi.ca/cihiweb.pdf

SECONDARY SOURCE: For information originally from a different source	**Citation in the body of your essay:** (as cited in Green, 2016) In instances where you use information and opinions that originally come from a different source, you must credit both the original author and the author of the article where you found the information: For example, according to the United Nations, "North Korea is the biggest threat to peace in Asia" (as cited in Green, 2016). Note: In this example, the United Nations made this statement, but we found it in an article by Green.

4.8 Reporting phrases for paraphrasing and quoting

Reporting phrases introduce quotations and paraphrases and acknowledge another author's ideas and information. If the wording is important, it is better to quote your source, but if it is the facts that are important, not the wording, it better to paraphrase. In either case, the way you introduce your evidence signifies to what extent you agree with it. Here are some expressions you can use to introduce information:

If you agree with what the writer says…	
The work of X indicates that …	As X has indicated, …
The work of X reveals that …	A study by X shows that …
Turning to X, one finds that …	X has drawn attention to the fact that …
In a study of Y, X found that …	X correctly argues that …
As X points out, …	X rightly points out that …

If you disagree with what the writer says…	
X claims that …	The work of X asserts that …
X states erroneously that …	X feels that …

If you do not want to give your point of view about what the writer says…	
According to X, …	X notes that …
It is the view of X that …	X states that …
The opinion of X is that …	X observes that …
Research by X suggests that …	X concludes that …
X reports that …	X argues that …

Quoting…	
As X said/says, "… …"	It was X who said, "… …"
As X stated/states, "… …"	According to X, "… …"
As X wrote/writes, "… …"	X claims, "… …"
As X pointed/points out, "… …"	X found, "… …"

Concluding…	
The evidence seems to indicate that…	Thus, it could be concluded that…
It must, therefore, be recognized that…	The evidence seems to be strong that…
The indications are, therefore, that…	On this basis, it may be inferred that…
It is clear, therefore, that …	Given this evidence, it can be seen that…

4.9 Model essay

Study the following example essay. Look carefully at how the essay has been organized and how the author has used evidence to support the points she makes.

The Hidden Costs of Advertising

The average person sees 4,000 to 10,000 advertisements every day (Marshall, 2015). Advertisements have been used as a form of persuasion since individuals, tribes, and societies first started trading products and services. Today, ads can be found in magazines, newspapers, or even on road-side signs. Furthermore, TV commercials and internet advertisements have increased with advancements in technology, so advertising has a huge impact on our lives, whether we are aware of it or not. Consequently, this essay will discuss the positives and negatives of advertising to then determine how beneficial it really is.

On the one hand, advertising has brought great benefits in industry as it has always been used to increase sales, and as a result, boost the economy. Modern technology has made it much easier for companies to reach millions of potential customers. Using Google AdWords, for instance, a company can generate $3 in sales for every $1.60 spent on advertising (Milenkovic, 2019). Furthermore, companies can increase demand by persuading new target markets to purchase their products or services, as a result, contributing even more to the company's profits and the economy. According to small business owner Jonathan Barnard "Local businesses are able to do a decent local online campaign and target new customers with just a few hundred dollars" (as cited in Weissbrot, 2019). Thus, advertising is very useful in terms of marketing products and services and driving economic growth.

On the other hand, adverts can have a number of negative impacts. In many other countries, roadside billboards can be enormous and extremely bright and distracting. For instance, a 2015 study by the University of Alabama recorded more billboards at crash sites (as cited in Sesto, 2018), indicating that this form of advertising can distract drivers and cause accidents. Moreover, another common drawback of advertising is that people are encouraged to purchase things that they don't actually need. The catchy slogan, "Live Richly" dreamed up by the Fallon Worldwide advertising agency, encouraged consumers to take out huge loans and then default on $10 billion in the 2007/8 financial crisis (as cited in Story, 2008). Clearly, therefore, advertising can have a direct impact on our physical safety but also our financial wellbeing.

To put this into perspective, I believe that the drawbacks outweigh the benefits. Despite the positive results for a company's sales and the economy as a whole, advertising also causes some terrible side effects. As a suggestion, advertisements should be limited and possibly reduced alongside roads to prevent distractions, but they should be allowed in limited situations so that customers can still be reached and businesses can still grow. However, advertising that encourages people to buy bad products or go into too much debt should definitely be regulated or completely banned.

References

Marshall, R. (2015, September 10). How many ads do you see in one day? Red Crow Marketing. https://www.redcrowmarketing.com/2015/09/10/

Milenkovic, M. (2019, July 31). The 45 most important advertising statistics of 2019. Small Biz Genius. smallbizgenius.net/by-the-numbers/advertising-statistics/

Sesto, G. (2018, July 2). Statistics on fatal accidents indicate correlation between digital billboards and traffic accidents. Dash Two. https://dashtwo.com/blog/statistics-on-fatal-accidents-indicate-no-correlation-with-traffic-accidents/

Story, L (2008, August 14). Home equity frenzy was a bank ad come true. New York Times. https://www.nytimes.com/2008/08/15/business/15sell/

Weissbrot, A. (2019, October 7). Zenith: Small business drives global ad spend growth and the duopoly reaps the rewards. Ad Exchanger. https://adexchanger.com/agencies/zenith-small-business-drives-global-ad-spend-growth-and-the-duopoly-reaps-the-rewards/

Notice that each supporting point in the essay has evidence to show how true or how strong each supporting point is. In addition, each item of evidence has a citation, and each citation has a corresponding reference at the end of the essay. Notice also that the references are in alphabetical order (Ma, Mi, Se, St, W), and that every line except the first line is indented.

Chapter 4: Using evidence

Now, complete the following reverse outline based on the previous essay *The Hidden Costs of Advertising*. You don't need to copy whole sentences.

The point of this exercise is to carefully consider and understand how the essay has been organized and supported.

PARAGRAPH 1 (Introduction)

    Hook:

_____

    Background/linking information (who what when where why):

_____

_____

_____

    Thesis statement:

_____

_____

PARAGRAPH 2 (Body paragraph 1)

    Main idea of the paragraph:

_____

    Supporting idea 1: _____

    Evidence for supporting idea 1:

_____

_____

    Supporting idea 2: _____

    Evidence for supporting idea 2:

_____

_____

Supporting idea 3: _____

Evidence for supporting idea 3 (if any):

_____

_____

PARAGRAPH 3 (Body paragraph 2)

Main idea of the paragraph:

_____

Supporting idea 1: _____

Evidence for supporting idea 1:

_____

_____

Supporting idea 2: _____

Evidence for supporting idea 2:

_____

_____

Supporting idea 3 (if any): _____

Evidence for supporting idea 3:

_____

_____

PARAGRAPH 4 (Conclusion)

_____

_____

4.10 Using evidence: practice 1

Here, you will see a selection of evidence on the topic of studying abroad together with the original sources of information below. Insert this evidence in the most appropriate places in the essay that follows. Remember to quote professional opinions but paraphrase facts. You should also include a correct citation and reporting phrase for each item of evidence.

EVIDENCE 1. Studying overseas can be one of the most enjoyable and life-changing opportunities that a student can have.

SOURCE 1. This opinion was expressed by York St. John University on their website https://www.yorksj.ac.uk/international/why-choose-ysj. The article is entitled Study in the UK, Change Your World but there is no publishing date on the website.

EVIDENCE 2. According to research by the International Institute of Education, the all-encompassing average cost of studying abroad in a foreign country hovers around $18,000 per semester, or $36,000 per full academic year.

SOURCE 2. This research was obtained from an article entitled How Much Does It Cost to Study Abroad? Written by Dominic James Fusco, July 11, 2017 for the website named Go Abroad. The original article is available at https://www.goabroad.com/articles/how-much-does-it-cost-to-study-abroad

---

EVIDENCE 3. Depression and anxiety among overseas students make life very difficult especially as they don't have their usual friends and family around them for support.

SOURCE 3. Holly Smith wrote the article Is Studying Abroad Dangerous? 4 Real Things to Consider. It was published by Student World Online and is available at http://www.studentworldonline.com/article/is-studying-abroad-dangerous

---

EVIDENCE 4. More than 4.3 million tertiary-level students were enrolled outside their country of citizenship in 2015.

SOURCE 4. This article entitled Education Levels and Student Numbers was published in 2016 by the Organization for Economic Co-operation and Development (OECD). Original article available at https://www.oecd-ilibrary.org/docserver/eag_highlights-2012-9-en.pdf

---

EVIDENCE 5. More than 80 percent of hiring managers feel that cross-cultural understanding and knowledge of a global marketplace are assets to the competitiveness of their companies.

SOURCE 5. Tim Johnson wrote this article for University Affairs entitled Why Do So Many Canadians Choose to Study Abroad? The article is available at https://www.universityaffairs.ca/features/study-abroad/

EVIDENCE 6. In the latest Programme for International Student Assessment (PISA) score results in 2016, Thailand is ranked 55th out of 72 countries in the overall results.

SOURCE 6. This article was written by Supakit Wiitiyasin and published in the International Journal for Integrated Educational Development in 2017. The original paper can be viewed at file:///C:/Users/user/Downloads/131930-Article-347863.pdf

GET IT WRITE! The Ultimate Guide to Academic Writing

Now read the following essay. Determine which evidence from the previous page best supports each point. Paraphrase or quote as most appropriate and include a correct reporting phrase and citation for each source. Remember, the goal here is to determine what point the writer is making and what evidence best proves that point.

Overseas Adventure

[Insert hook here: _____

_____

_____]. As technology and transportation have improved, more young people than ever before are flying hundreds or thousands of miles away to pursue their education abroad. This sounds like a great adventure, but there are also some important risks to be considered before opting for this path in life. Therefore, to better understand the pros and cons of studying abroad, this essay will analyze both sides before drawing a conclusion.

First of all, there are a few obvious benefits to be obtained from learning in a foreign country. The most obvious advantage is the better quality of education that is available in developed nations, especially if students come from countries with a relatively poor education system. [Insert evidence here: _____

_____

_____]. As a result, if they are lucky enough to get the opportunity, they can significantly improve their education and obtain much better prospects in life. Moreover, the independence that these young people have to deal with ensures that they can also develop socially and emotionally. [Insert evidence here: _____

_____

_____]. In other words, what they learn outside the classroom can be just as valuable as what they learn

134

inside the classroom, and this certainly helps them to become more independent. As a result, the students who have overseas experience are highly sought after in the job market. [Insert evidence here: _____

_____

_____]. Clearly, the quality of education, worldly experience, and future prospects are the main benefits of studying abroad.

On the other hand, there are downsides that should not be taken lightly or ignored. The first is the cost. Studying abroad is always more expensive than learning in their own country. [Insert evidence here: _____

_____

_____]. There are ways to mitigate the expense such as grants and scholarships, but there is no escaping the fact that it is certainly more expensive to study abroad. The other important aspect to consider is the increased stress that students encounter living abroad on their own. [Insert evidence here: _____

_____

_____]. In other words, students are under increased stress because they are alone in a foreign country, but this is made worse by the lack of support that they have. Therefore, there are certainly a few negatives to consider before jumping on an airplane.

Considering all of the arguments and evidence above, it seems reasonable to conclude that it is certainly not an easy decision. The benefits in terms of the higher standard of education and future opportunities seem clear. However, the cost and potential stress should not be overlooked. If parents research carefully and apply for grants and scholarships, the cost can be reduced, but the stress is much harder to prevent.

I would suggest that it partly depends on the character of the student. If they are adventurous and independent, maybe studying abroad would suit their character, but for quieter, less outgoing students, I think it would be better to stay closer to home.

Now, look back again at the source information that was provided for each item of evidence and write correctly ordered and formatted references for the essay. Remember to organize your references alphabetically and indent every line after the first line (opposite to how you indent paragraphs).

References

_____

_____

_____

_____

_____

_____

_____

_____

_____

_____

_____

_____

_____

4.11 Using evidence: practice 2

Read the following paragraph about pollution and label each sentence as (C) if it is specific information or an expert opinion that requires a citation, or (NC) if it is common knowledge and does not require a citation.

Our Choking Planet

By Dr. Steven Bush, February 12, 2016

Pollution has become an increasingly concerning issue in recent years (___). When we speak of pollution, most people automatically think of air pollution (___). However, pollution is much more than that (___). Indeed, having researched this topic for so many years, I would define pollution as the release of any substance or thing into the environment that is harmful for human, animal, and plant life (___). Therefore, pollution is not just dirty air (___). Water pollution refers to the contamination of water bodies such as seas, lakes, and oceans when pollutants are discharged into water without proper treatment (___). Indeed, every day, two million tons of sewage and industrial and agricultural waste are discharged into the world's water, which is equivalent to the combined weight of the world's entire human population (___). Air pollution is another serious problem that damages environmental balance and causes several diseases (___). The major causes include deforestation and the burning of fuels (___). A recent report by the World Health Organization states that an average of 2 million people are killed worldwide every year due to air pollution (___). Noise pollution is also a common problem, especially in cities (___). The WHO guidelines for community noise recommend less than 30 decibels (dB(A)) in bedrooms for good quality sleep and less than 35 dB(A) in classrooms to allow good learning conditions (___). However, according to a European Union (EU) publication, about 40% of the population in EU countries is exposed to road traffic noise at levels exceeding 55 db(A) (___). The principal cause behind all this pollution is our exploitation of nature (___). The environmental laws across the globe attempt to control pollution, but many people and businesses ignore the law if it is not in their interests (___). However, since we caused the problem, we're also responsible for solving the problem (___).

Now, use the most appropriate evidence from the previous paragraph to support the statements below. Pretend that the five statements are statements that you have made in an essay that you are writing about global pollution, and you would like to use evidence from the previous paragraph *Our Choking Planet* to support your own opinions on the subject. Be sure to paraphrase or quote as appropriate and include an appropriate citation and/or reporting phrase each time.

1. Many people oversimplify pollution and think only of dirty air.

    Example Answer: However, pollution is actually "the release of any substance into the environment that is harmful for human, animal, and plant life" (Bush, 2016).

    OR

    In fact, Bush (2016) points out that pollution is actually "the release of any substance or thing into the environment that is harmful for human, animal, and plant life."

2. Society must work together to solve the problem of pollution.

3. Water pollution is worse than most people realize.

4. The risks of noise pollution are often underestimated by people.

5. Air pollution can be dangerous for people's health.

4.12 Using evidence: practice 3

Read the following example news stories and use the most appropriate information or opinions correctly formatted as evidence to support the paragraphs that follow.

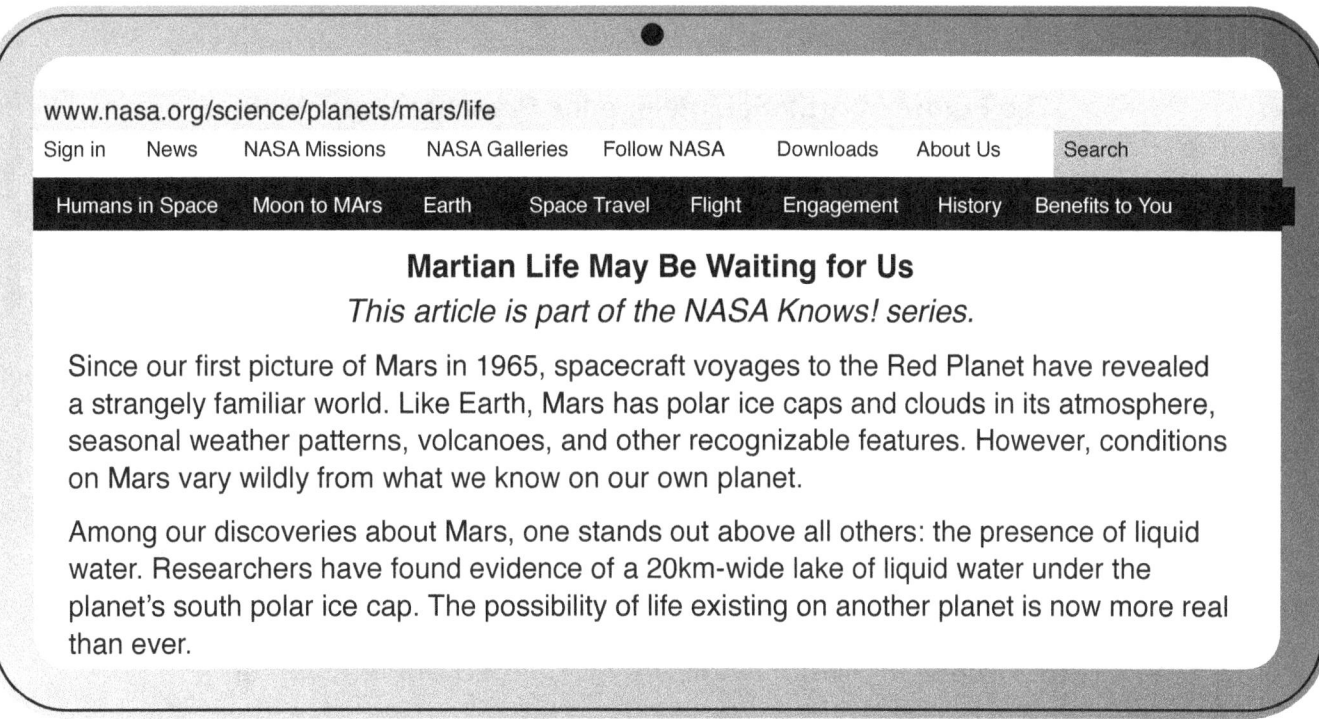

Now complete the following student paragraph using the most appropriate evidence from the news story above and write a correctly formatted reference after.

Mars has fascinated us since we first watched the red planet moving through the sky in a pattern that didn't match the other stars. People have often wondered if there might be other life out there, and Mars may offer us the best chance of finding life as the planet may have the essential factor for life — water. Indeed, there is now strong evidence that Mars contains vast amounts of water in its polar regions and frozen beneath its dusty surface. [Insert evidence here: _____

_____

_____]. As a result, it seems quite optimistic that we may find evidence for life outside of the Earth.

Reference

_____

_____

GET IT WRITE! *The Ultimate Guide to Academic Writing*

---

www.wwnnews.com/science/thefutureofai

Sign in News Sport Weather Environment Travel More   Search

WWN NEWS

World Europe America Asia Africa Business Tech Health Entertainmant More

The Future of Artificial Intelligence Presents Great Risk

August 4, 2015

Recent developments in engineering have resulted in some amazing developments in computing power and artificial intelligence — thinking robots. The World Health Organization has said that robots may be able to provide the care that aging populations need as well as many other advantages. This may well be true, but the risks of artificial intelligence make it far more dangerous than most people imagine. Professor Stephen Hawking has even said that "Robots may mean the end of humanity."

Now complete the following student paragraph using the most appropriate evidence from the news story above and write a correctly formatted reference after.

Technology has been relentlessly developing for centuries, and the next momentous event on the horizon is artificial intelligence, also known as AI. Despite the often-cited benefits, the creation of truly intelligent machines that can think for themselves could actually pose the greatest danger to our society. [Insert evidence here: _____

_____

_____

_____]. If one of the most respected scientists in the world is worried about AI, then maybe we should also consider how we progress with our technology a little more carefully.

Reference

_____

_____

Chapter 4: Using evidence

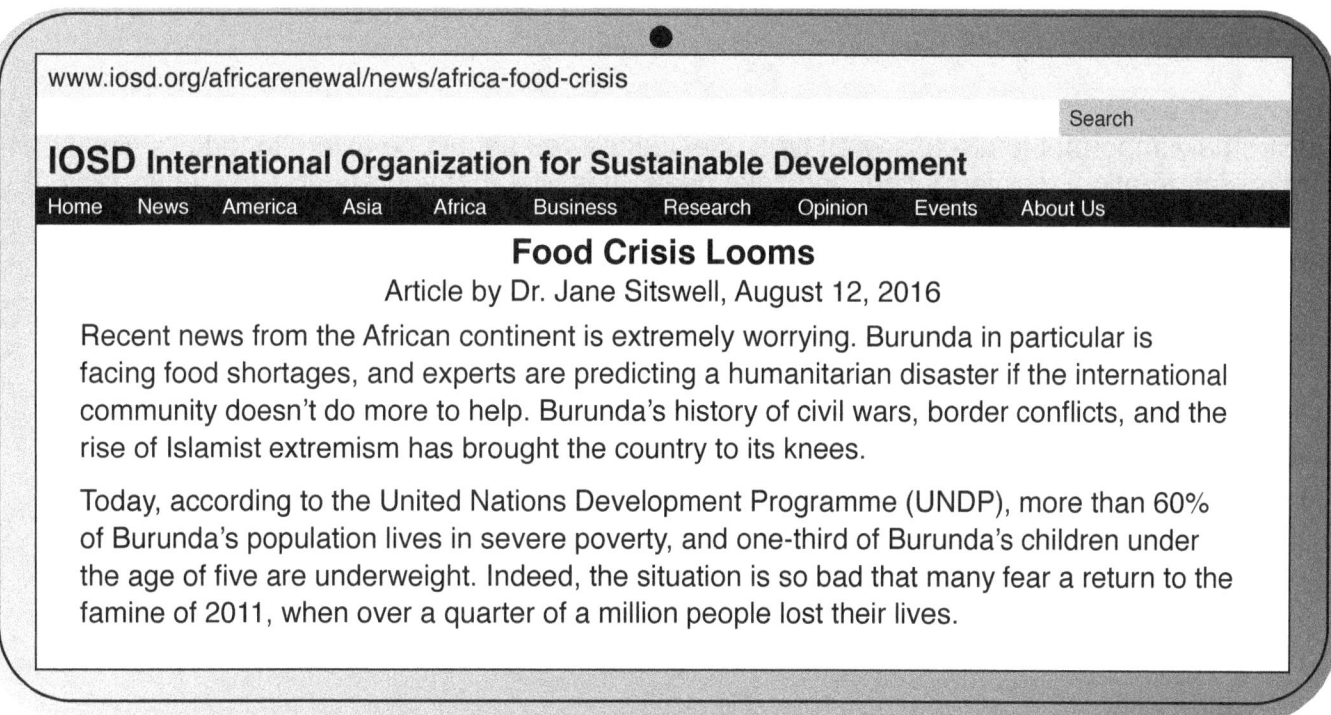

Now complete the following student paragraph using the most appropriate evidence from the news story above and write a correctly formatted reference after.

Africa again seems to be facing disastrous consequences or war, political instability and global warming. The African continent just can't seem to escape these seemingly constant obstacles to peace. One country that is once again in the news is Burunda. Decades of war, poverty, and Muslim extremism has brought the country once again to the brink of disaster. People are struggling just to survive. [Insert evidence here: _____ _____ _____]. Indeed, the situation is so bad that many are calling for the international community to urgently do more, or millions may die of starvation.

Reference

_____

_____

4.13 Source analysis

Now that we have discussed how to correctly incorporate evidence into your writing, it is also extremely important to discuss what type of evidence you should be using. In today's world of misinformation, disinformation, and 'fake news', it is vital that you are able to identify bias and misleading information. Modern information technology makes it very easy to produce professional-looking websites and videos, but good research is about determining the truth. It is *not* about finding evidence to support what you *think* is true or what you *want* to be true. As you research, you should look for the following:

1. Source

Who wrote the article or produced the video? Is he or she an expert in the field with the knowledge and experience to make informed and reliable comments on a specific topic? What organization or publisher is behind the information? Is it a news website, a blog, a non-profit organization, a business, a political party, or an academic organization? How easy is it to determine this information? If this type of information has been hidden or made purposely difficult to find, why do you think they would do this?

2. Timeliness

Our knowledge and understanding of the world evolves over time. 'Facts' change. It is not so long ago that most people accepted as 'fact' that the earth was the center of the universe, and that disease was caused by the devil. As you research, you want to discover the truth of the situation *today*. Therefore, it is important to use the most current and up-to-date information available.

3. Evidence

What evidence is provided and where does the evidence come from? How much evidence is provided, and what is the quality of this evidence? Similar to number 1 above, evidence should come from reliable sources that can be trusted to provide accurate and complete information on a given topic. If the source does not provide any evidence for their claims or the evidence is highly questionable, then you should probably ignore the source.

4. Bias

A good source of information will always attempt to present a balanced and fair assessment of a topic, based on a correct and complete understanding of all the relevant facts. We all have biases of some form or another — it is human nature. However, good research should avoid bias and stick to the facts. Without the truth, we cannot form the right opinions or make the right decisions. If you can see that a source is not being fair in the way they present and support a topic, then you should ignore that source. If a source is biased, they often seek to present and support just their side of the issue, but they also use loaded language in order to elicit an emotional response from the audience and manipulate people's opinions and actions.

5. Purpose

Compared to the oceans of information that we have available to us at the click of a mouse, there are actually very few sources of information that are not motivated by ideological or economic drivers. Many news outlets, websites, social media influencers, political leaders, and 'experts' have an agenda of their own, and they often seek to use their influence to manipulate society into adopting their ideology or purchasing the product or service that they stand to benefit from. As you research, look carefully at the information and ideas that a source presents and determine if the source is making an honest attempt to share a complete and factual assessment of the topic.

Chapter 4: Using evidence

Compare the two news article excerpts below. Both articles deal with the same story, but notice how they deal with the same story differently. Analyze the articles using the five keys to source analysis from the previous page. Which article is the most reliable?

---

www.wwnnews.com/politics/immigrantinvasion

Sign in | News | Sport | Weather | Environment | Travel | More | Search

WWN NEWS

World | Europe | America | Asia | Africa | Business | Tech | Health | Entertainmant | More

Immigrants Flooding in to Take Our Jobs Cause Chaos

by Staff Writer. Published 2 days ago

Last week, we reported on the floods of uneducated and criminal immigrants pouring into our country and the president's apparent unwillingness to protect the safety and livelihood of hard-working citizens like you and me. Since our initial report, tens of thousands more have crossed our borders, bringing all their problems and expecting the good people of this country to give them a free ride.

True patriots know what it means to work hard and pay taxes all our lives, and we all work hard to make this country what it is, so why on earth should we allow our weak and ineffectve government to allow this plague of the worst of humanity to infest our country?

Experts say this invasion could take valuable jobs away from our children and ruin the economy. We must act now to prevent disaster!

> LOVE YOUR COUNTRY AND WANT TO HELP?
> CLICK HERE TO SHOW YOUR PRIDE AND SUPPORT THE CAUSE...

Sponsored by the Federation for Conservative Principles

---

www.bluedotnews.com/politics/immigrationupdates

Sign in | News | Sport | Weather | Environment | Travel | More | Search

BLUEDOT NEWS

World | Europe | America | Asia | Africa | Business | Tech | Health | Entertainmant | More

Jump in Immigration due to Ongoing Turmoil

by Sarah Green, senior political editor. Published 2 days ago

Last week, the government reported that immigration has increased 13% on the previous year as ongoing corruption and organized crime in neighbouring countries have caused an estimated 11,000 deaths and caused hundreds of thousands to flee with their families in search of protection and safety.

Government spokesperson Lisa Perkowsky yesterday informed the nation that the president has ordered an extra 10,000 beds and an additional 1,000 border protection staff to be sent to help with processing and vetting in order to speed up the immigration process and prevent undesirable/unqualified people from entering.

Immigration is clearly a hot topic at the moment, but the president Tweeted yesterday that "We are in a position to help our neighbours and do the right thing, but we must proceed quickly and carefully."

> LOVE THE NEWS AND WANT TO UNDERSTAND CURRENT AFFAIRS?
> CLICK HERE TO SIGN UP FOR FREE DAILY UPDATES...

4.14 Grammar check 4

Read the following referenced essay and circle the correct answers. As you read, study the type of essay and the way in which evidence has been used. Be prepared to explain your answers. Note that because this is a referenced essay, it also contains citations in bold font, but please ignore these as you read for correct grammar choices.

Slowed Down by Fast Food

Dr. Mathew Straw from Walter Evans University said, "A couple of lettuce leaves in your burger does not make it a balanced diet" **(as cited in Food Facts, 2018)**. As (*social, society*) has developed, (*every, Ø, most*) people have less time to cook meals. (*As a result, Because, So*), companies developed processed foods that require less time and effort to prepare. (*But, Even though, However*), fast food often contains additional ingredients to give (*them, it*) extra flavor and a longer shelf life, (*which, that, this*) has caused a lot of controversy. As this is (*a, the*) significant issue in today's world, (*so, Ø*) this essay will discuss (*Ø, the*) advantages and disadvantages of fast food in order to determine its true value.

On the one hand, there are some significant advantages (*Ø, that*) should not (*overlook, be overlooked*). One of the most important benefits (*are, is*) the time that people can (*safe, safety, save*). Life seems busier (*in the present, these days*), and most (*adults have, adult has*) less time to do (*chore, chores*) at home. According to Pew Research **(Patten, 2015)**, (*it says that, Ø*) in nearly half of two-parent households, both parents (*work, worked*) full time. (*This, That, It*) means that families need quick and (*convenient, convenience*) meals, and most fast food from (*a, the, Ø*) restaurants and stores (*are, is*) ready to eat in just a few minutes. Furthermore, (*the, Ø*) another advantage is (*Ø, a, the*) price of fast food as meals are often (*more cheap, cheaper, more cheaper*) than handmade meals. For instance, McDonald's recently (*introduced, introducing, introduces*) a $1, $2, and $3 menu (*for attracting, to attract*) more low-income (*customers, customer*) **(Lufkin, 2018)**. Clearly, the time and money that can (*save, be saved*) can make fast food (*to be, be, Ø*) attractive to many people.

On the (*another, other*) hand, fast food also has some downsides. One of (*this, these*) is the obesity that affects (*to, Ø*) many people these days. Of course, there are other factors such as (*they lack, a lack of*) exercise, (*however, but*) this public health problem is also partly (*because, due to*) the quality of food that people consume. As Dr. Ananya **Mandal (2019)** states, (*in, Ø*) fast foods are usually high in calories, fats, and (*have, Ø*) sugar, which (*Ø, they*) cause people to gain weight. Another issue is (*a, the, Ø*) quantity of fast food that people (*consume, consumed*). (*Someone, Many people, People*) eat a lot more these days (*because of, because*) fast food is so cheap, (*tasty, tastes good*), and (*convenience, convenient*). (*In a, A*) study by **Harvard T.**

H. Chan School of Public Health (n.d.) found that people (*give, are given*) bigger portions these days, and they (*consistently, consistent*) eat more (*even if, even*) they are already full. The final drawback is the long-term effects of the additional (*ingredients, ingredient*) that (*add, are added*) to fast food. A lot of fast food (*is contain, contains*) chemicals such as sodium nitrate and potassium bromate, which (*are, is*) used to increase flavour and shelf life, (*however, but, Ø*) these chemicals have been linked to serious health problems **(Shkodzik, n.d.)**. (*Therefore, So, However*), it seems that fast food has some (*concerned, concerning*) impacts that people should (*be, Ø*) aware of.

In conclusion, there are clearly (*Ø, have*) many factors to consider (*if, when, during*) people choose their meals. The cheap prices and convenience (*is, are*) obviously important for many people in modern society, (*in contrast, but, conversely*) I (*Ø, am*) strongly believe that the dangers of fast food (*are, is*) too (*significance, significant*) to ignore. People should (*strict, be strict with*) their diet and avoid (*to eat, eating*) fast food as much as possible (*despite, because, due to*) the health concerns that (*cause, are caused*) by this heavily processed type of food.

Note: In the references, rather than select the correct option from a range of choices, please identify and correct any mistakes.

Reference

Straw, M. (n.d.). The meaning of a balanced diet in the 21st century.
https://www.foodfacts.org/obesity-prevention-source/the-meaning-of-balanced-diet/

Food Facts (2018). The meaning of a balanced diet in the 21st century.
https://www.foodfacts.org/obesity-prevention-source/the-meaning-of-balanced-diet/

Harvard T. H. Chan School of Public Health (N.D.). Obesity prevention source.
https://www.hsph.harvard.edu/obesity-prevention-source/obesity-causes/diet-and-weight/

News Medical (2019, February 27). Obesity and fast food. Ananya Mandal.
https://www.news-medical.net/health/Obesity-and-Fast-Food.aspx

Shkodzik, K. (n.d.). What's in Fast Food? The Truth about Fast Food Ingredients. FloHealth.
https://flo.health/menstrual-cycle/lifestyle/diet-and-nutrition/the-truth-about-ingredients

Patten, E. (November 4, 2015). How American parents balance work and family life when both work. Pew research center.
https://www.pewresearch.org/fact-tank/2015/11/04/how-american-parents-balance-work-and-family-life-when-both-work/

4.15 Writing practice

Choose one of the topics below to write a discursive (compare/contrast) essay using evidence from the internet to support your ideas. As you research, be sure to choose reliable sources of factual and reliable information, identify the main issues involved, and select the strongest pieces of evidence that you might wish to use to support the different points that you raise in your essay.

Once you have identified the main arguments and the evidence you wish to use, be sure to paraphrase or quote the evidence as appropriate. Finally, make sure you have a citation and matching reference for each and every piece of evidence in your essay.

Once you have selected a topic that would like to write about, use the advantages and disadvantages table on page 147 to help you brainstorm both sides of each issue.

There is also an outline for you to follow after the brainstorming table. Make sure you brainstorm and plan your essay first. This is essential for a well-organized, well-developed, and well-supported essay.

1. Should gambling be legal? Discuss both sides of the argument before choosing whether or not to support gambling.

2. Do you agree that lying is sometimes acceptable? Discuss both sides of the argument before choosing whether or not to support lying.

3. Should the government pedestrianize certain areas of your city by banning all vehicles? Discuss both sides of the argument before choosing whether or not to support pedestrianization.

4. Do you think people who drive cars should be forced to pay a pollution tax? Discuss both sides of the argument before choosing whether or not to support one side or the other.

5. Do you think begging should be banned in cities? Discuss both sides of the argument before choosing whether or not to support one side or the other.

6. Do you think prostitution should be legal? Discuss both sides of the argument before choosing whether or not to support prostitution.

7. Do you think sports should be part of a school's curriculum? Discuss both sides of the argument before choosing whether or not to support sports in school.

8. Should animals be used for research? Discuss both sides of the argument before choosing whether or not to support animal testing.

9. Is cosmetic surgery a positive or a negative social trend? Discuss both sides of the argument before choosing whether or not to support cosmetic surgery.

10. Should your country raise the legal drink age? Discuss both sides of the argument before choosing whether or not to support a higher legal drinking age.

Chapter 4: Using evidence

Use the table below to brainstorm ideas. Remember — do not write sentences and do not worry about spelling or whether something is a good or a bad idea at the this stage. Just note down as many ideas as you can, as quickly as you can.

Topic to brainstorm	
Advantages	Disadvantages
1.	1.
2.	2.
3.	3.
4.	4.
5.	5.
6.	6.
7.	7.
8.	8.
9.	9.
10.	10.

On the next page, you will construct an outline in which you group and support your ideas in separate paragraphs. Remember — it is still your essay with *your* main ideas, *your* opinions, and *your* explanations, but you must also include evidence to show how true and how strong your different ideas are.

As you research, find good sources of information, keep track of the websites that you use, include an appropriate citation with each and every piece of evidence, and provide a list of corresponding references at the end of your essay.

4.16 Essay outline

Now group and support your ideas using the outline below to help you organize your ideas before you write a referenced discursive essay.

 There is a version of this outline available in the supporting online material.

PARAGRAPH 1 (Introduction)

Hook: _____

_____

Background/linking information (who what when where why):

_____

_____

_____

Thesis statement:

_____

_____

PARAGRAPH 2 (Body paragraph 1)

Main idea of the paragraph:

_____

Supporting idea 1:

_____

Evidence for supporting idea 1:

_____

_____

Supporting idea 2:

_____

Evidence for supporting idea 2:

_____

_____

Supporting idea 3 (optional):
___

Evidence for supporting idea 3 (if any):
___
___

PARAGRAPH 3 (Body paragraph 2)

Main idea of the paragraph:
___

Supporting idea 1:
___

Evidence for supporting idea 1:
___
___

Supporting idea 2:
___

Evidence for supporting idea 2:
___
___

Supporting idea 3 (optional):
___

Evidence for supporting idea 3 (if any):
___
___

PARAGRAPH 4 (Conclusion)

___
___

4.17 Essay checklist

Once you have written your essay, use the following checklist to make sure you have all the correct components. You should answer 'yes' to all of the questions if you have organised, supported, and formatted your essay correctly.

1. Is there a title (a correctly capitalized noun phrase, not a sentence)

2. Is there a hook (an interesting observation, question, statistic, or "quote") related to the topic to grab the reader's attention?

3. Does the hook have a correct reporting phrase and citation?

4. Is there interesting and relevant background information? W.W.W.W.W. + H. — what exactly is the topic? Who does it affect? Where and when does is happen? Why is this an important issue? How did this issue develop and become so important?

5. Is there a thesis statement that introduces the topic of the essay and the fact that the essay will be looking at both sides of the issue?

6. Does each body paragraph have a clear topic sentence introducing one side of the debate or the other?

7. Does each body paragraph have at least two different supporting ideas that relate to and support the main idea of the paragraph?

8. Is there evidence to support each of the arguments for and against the topic?

9. Has all the evidence been paraphrased or quoted appropriately? Remember that opinions and definitions should be "quoted", but facts and statistics should be paraphrased. Don't quote everything, and don't copy anything! Try submitting your essay to Turnitin.com. If you have never used this website, you will need to register. Once you have signed up, use class id 27620195 and enrollment key GetItWrite! (all one word with a capital G, capital I (i), and capital W, with an exclamation mark (!) at the end) to submit your essay and see if there is any plagiarism (copying/cheating). Note, however, that quotes, proper nouns (names), and most or all of your references will be highlighted, but this is normal and not a problem. What is *not* acceptable, however, is whole sentences or copied chunks of sentences that are highlighted but not in quote marks (" ") — this is plagiarism and can harm both your grade and your professional reputation.

10. Does all evidence have a correct reporting phrase and APA citation?

11. Do the body paragraphs have a conclusion? If a paragraph ends on quite a specific point or evidence, then it is nice to add a conclusion to remind the reader what big idea the paragraph is attempting to prove.

12. Are the paragraphs long enough? Each body paragraph should have a topic sentence, at least two supporting ideas (three or even four would be better), evidence

to support each point, and a conclusion, so these paragraphs should have at least six sentences. However, if the writer has done a good job of developing and explaining their ideas then a strong (high scoring) paragraph should have seven or eight sentences.

13. Does the essay have a conclusion that restates the main points covered (not copied from the thesis statement), and does the conclusion also include a prediction about the future or a recommendation for those affected by the issue?

14. Does Command/Control F reveal a good range or vocabulary (not too much repetition of key words)?

15. Did you avoid saying 'you' and 'I' in your essay? Remember, you should *never* say 'you' as you do not know who will read your essay, and you should generally avoid saying 'I' unless the essay prompt asks for your opinion about something. Even then, saying 'I' is best left for introductions and conclusions; body paragraphs should focus on factual information rather than personal reflection.

16. Is punctuation correct throughout the essay, with capital letters only being used at the very start of each sentence and for all proper nouns, and is there a space after all full stops and commas?

17. Does the essay have a correctly formatted list of references at the end?

18. Do the references match the citations?

19. Are the references in alphabetical order?

20. Is the essay correctly formatted according to your teacher's instructions? For instance, double-spaced Times New Roman 12-point font.

 Let's see how much you understand and remember from Chapters 1 to 4. Take the Grammar Review and Final APA Test in the supporting online material.